What People Are Saying About
Opening to Love 365 Days a Year

"Don't be deceived by the apparent simplicity of this book. It provides practical wisdom about the things that matter to us all. Notice the complexity of emotion offered in the daily meditations. We all need direct uncomplicated guidance to love well in our complicated lives."

—**Thomas Moore**
author, *Care of the Soul* and *Original Self*

"True, passionate, lasting love is a 365-day-a-year adventure. Every person who wants a fantastic relationship owes it to themselves to read and remember the wisdom this book offers."

—**Michael Webb**
author, *The RoMANtic's Guide: Hundreds of Creative Tips for a Lifetime of Love*

"I recommend this book for all lovers and all those who are seeking love. *Opening to Love 365 Days a Year* was obviously written by two warm, tender and caring Sweet Spirits."

—**Kenny Kingston**
legendary celebrity psychic

"*Opening to Love 365 Days a Year* is a great way to start each morning and end each evening. Whether you're single, dating, in a committed relationship or married, these pearls of wisdom will surely add a joyful smile to your lips and pleasant laughter to your heart. Drs. Judith and Jim have created a romantic winner!"

—**Dr. Grace Cornish**
author, *10 Bad Choices That Ruin Black Women's Lives*

"Here is a delightful bouquet of recipes for heartful living. A refreshing dose of inspiration for every day of the year."

—**Joyce Vissell, R.N., M.S. and Barry Vissell, M.D.**
authors, *The Shared Heart* and *The Heart's Wisdom*

Opening to Love 365 Days a Year

JUDITH SHERVEN, Ph.D.

JAMES SNIECHOWSKI, Ph.D.

Health Communications, Inc.
Deerfield Beach, Florida

www.hci-online.com

To foster the celebration differences, a percentage of the proceeds from the sale of this book will be donated to organizations that promote respect and value for differences.

Library of Congress Cataloging-in-Publication Data

Sherven, Judith.
    Opening to love 365 days a year / Judith Sherven, James Sniechowski.
      p.   cm.
    ISBN 1-55874-745-1
    1. Love—Miscellanea.   2. Couples—Miscellanea.   3. Marriage—
Miscellanea.   4. Affirmations.   I. Sniechowski, James.   II. Title.
HQ801.S5246   2000
306.7—dc21   99-048223
                                             CIP

Publisher: Health Communications, Inc.
               3201 S.W. 15th Street
               Deerfield Beach, FL 33442-8190

Cover and inside book design by Lawna Patterson Oldfield

Dedicated to
valuing and respecting
"The Magic of Differences"
between us.

In memory of all who
have lost their lives to violence,
which is always the result of fear and
hatred of differences.

The future of the world will not be determined between nations, but, rather, in the relationship between men and women.

D. H. LAWRENCE

Reader's Guide

Our Appreciation

We are delighted that Peter Vegso, president of Health Communications, Inc., invited us to write this book. Thank you, Peter, for the opportunity to share the joyous pleasure of conscious loving in this handy, easy-to-follow format. Writing *Opening to Love 365 Days a Year* has been a very special experience in our lives, almost as though we were being guided in our choices and in our writing.

Thank you Christine Belleris and Allison Janse, our very helpful, supportive and enthusiastic editors. It's been a pleasure to work with you both again. We also want to express our gratitude to Lawna Patterson Oldfield, the artistic designer for this book.

And thank you to the whole staff at Health Communications, Inc., for your consistent support and encouragement for our first book—*The New Intimacy: Discovering the Magic at the Heart of Your Differences.* Please know how deeply we appreciate your efforts on our behalf.

Thank you to our agent, Jan Miller, and everyone in her

office for their responsiveness and creativity on our behalf.

We thank Peg Booth and Kris Clegg, our enthusiastic publicists, for their wonderful promotion of *The New Intimacy*.

And we want to express our gratitude to the friends who participated in helping us with some of the quotes in the book. Your creativity and generosity of spirit has been delightfully entertaining, very moving and deeply appreciated.

Introduction

We've written *Opening to Love 365 Days a Year* because
we know that most people never receive any meaningful training or preparation for enjoyable, effective dating, or for creating a healthy and vital marriage. Our
national divorce rate is painful evidence of what follows
when people don't know how to be with one another in a
way that enriches them as individuals and as a couple, that
draws them closer and closer over time.

Opening to Love 365 Days a Year is our invitation to you
to become:

- more available to give love;
- more available to receive love;
- more determined to leave old wounds behind so you
  can live in the unfolding mystery of your future;
- more confident that you know how to address whatever
  needs attention so your life and your love can flourish.

Each of the following affirmations addresses a significant

aspect of dating and marriage: conflict, romance, trust, responsibility, commitment, self-respect, curiosity, celebration, frustration, companionship, sexuality and many, many more.

They are effective meditations that can help you to:

- increase your awareness of particular relationship concerns;
- change your mind from doubt and self-denial to optimism and self-respect;
- become far more available in the creation of a loving partnership.

You can learn to:

- handle conflicts in a loving and healthy manner;
- heal old wounds that often make loving a frightening experience;
- open to receive the love and attention that is given you in all areas of your life—a surprisingly difficult issue for so many people.

And you can have all this whether you're currently looking, already in a committed relationship or needing to change and repair a relationship that has been neglected or nearly destroyed.

How to Use These Affirmations

You can use these affirmations in any way you choose:

- As a daily reading that corresponds to the calendar, using the issue of the day as your meditation on practical, spiritually enriching love. Focusing on that day's issue, you can keep it in mind, write about it, talk about it, practice some new behavior or use all of these ways to become more available to yourself and to love.

• Turn to specific affirmations that are listed in the Reader's Guide, which relate to specific concerns you might be struggling with or needing support for on a particular day.

• Choose a page at random and trust that the content best fits your needs at the moment.

• Read *Opening to Love 365 Days a Year* as you would any regular book and practice whatever most appeals to you at the time. You may want to re-read certain sections of the book from time to time for the specific support you need to create more room in your heart for love. You may read it to redefine the differences between you and others as catalysts for greater understanding and richer romance. Or you may read it to take action toward giving and receiving love's gifts.

Of course, the more you do, the more you'll get what you desire.

Remember, your life belongs to you. It is yours to shape and create. Open to love. Open to life. *Opening to Love 365 Days a Year* is designed to help you do just that.

Our wish for you is that
You will be loved for all that you are
And love someone in just the same way!

To Make It Easier

In the following affirmations we most often use the terms "spouse," "lover" or "partner" for simplicity's sake. However, many of the affirmations also apply to a relationship with a date, friend, colleague or even your child.

Opening to Love can be useful whether you are married, dating, looking, separated, divorced, widowed, homosexual or heterosexual.

Destructive Differences

Throughout the following affirmations we will be inviting you to change your vision of the differences between you and your spouse, date, lover, partner—to open yourself to the value of differences.

IMPORTANT NOTE: *At no time are we condoning behaviors that are abusive or destructive—whether expressed emotionally or physically. Destructive differences are unacceptable and cannot be tolerated.*

January

If enough of us can rise to the current challenges of the man-woman relationship, using them as opportunities to peel away illusions, tap our deepest powers, and expand our sense of who we are, we can begin to develop the wisdom our age is lacking.

ABRAHAM MASLOW

The beginning of a new year is always a good time to set new goals, change our ways and make a deeper commitment to love. Whether in a relationship or single, each of us wants to be loved for all that we are and love someone in just the same way.

How can you do it better? How can you open yourself beyond what you already know?

First and foremost, remember that the other person is not you. While that may sound overly simplistic, most relationships fall apart over fights resulting from ignorance about this truth. When you unconsciously imagine that your lover is like you, then any disagreement is shocking. Every fight has to be won.

But when you can remember that your partner's feelings, beliefs and behaviors are just as important and valid as yours are, then you start off with the possibility of building a passionate, successful love between equals. Go for it!

I welcome new opportunities for love.

❧

A new year is a clean slate, a chance to suck in your breath, decide all is not lost and give yourself another chance.

Sarah Overstreet

More and more people want the experience of spirituality in their lives. But what does that mean? The simplest definition makes it something you can experience every day. When you are conscious of other people's lives having just as much value as yours, when you realize that every one of us was created by the same Source, then you are in the expansive awareness called *spiritual.*

When you live your marriage and love your spouse as a daily meditation on practical spirituality, you make choices and express yourself according to what is best for both of you. You realize that you are an instrument of God's abundance and to give is spiritual grace. You receive what is given you, because to reject the gift would be to reject the hand of God.

Commit to loving as a gift to you both, a gift of practical spirituality to All That Is.

Loving my spouse is practical spirituality.

❧

We must stop to observe ourselves
before we make decisions or take action, in order
to determine whether we were acting from a position of
fear and our need to be in control, or from a place
of love where we did what was right
for everyone involved.

Jim Britt

You took Math and Reading when you were in school. But you didn't have to take Communication Skills, Conflict Resolution, Respect for Personal Differences or Positive Parenting. And yet, you're allowed to get a marriage license and have children—with no preparation for the two most challenging and difficult experiences in life.

It's no wonder that most everyone hates to date, feels threatened by intimacy and fights in the most brutal and destructive ways. Where would we have learned otherwise? We copy our parents, we mimic the movies, we get advice from friends—hoping to be more successful.

The fact is, every one of us deserves compassion for our struggle to love well. With no training in even the basic skills, we need to feel more compassion for ourselves (and for everyone else). Today, be kind to yourself and your partner by remaining aware that you never took a class in even Relationship Basics and that you are learning as you go.

I deserve compassion for all I don't know.

*The ability to disagree with somebody but still respect them . . .
that's not something we're taught anymore.*

James Finn Garner

Right from the first moment you met, when you both began teaching each other how you expected the relationship to be, you were co-creating your relationship. Like a work of art, you jointly shaped what you now have. You are responsible for your choices and therein awaits your power.

If you don't like how your marriage works, it will take both of you to change and re-create it. If one of you won't do that, you don't really have a relationship—because real love requires both of you to be involved.

Intimacy is like a dance. It always takes both of you to co-create the steps you agree to take together. Today, agree to co-create something a bit different than you're used to. Perhaps you'll decide to take a walk after dinner holding hands or describe to each other when you felt the most happy in your life. You must create the intimacy of your marriage together.

I know that lasting love is co-created.

❧

It takes two people working together
to make a marriage work.

Abigail Van Buren (Dear Abby)

Lots of people imagine that when they love someone they will feel that rich, warm passion every minute of the day. They believe that they will never feel angry or bored or doubtful. But that's simply not true.

Loving someone is a journey that spans the gamut of human emotions and life experiences. If we were bedazzled every waking minute, we'd never be able to attend to a sick child or conduct a business meeting. We'd never sleep or gaze at the stars. Lasting love is ultimately a commitment, a choice to continue loving someone "through good times and bad, sickness and health."

Throughout your activities today, check in with yourself from time to time. Notice whether or not you are thinking about your beloved, or feeling loving feelings. If so, fine. If not, does the lack of loving focus mean you've lost interest? You want to move on to someone else? Probably not. Chances are, it just means your attention is on your day's events. Period.

I know I won't feel love all the time.

When you love someone you do not
love them all the time, in exactly the same way, from
moment to moment. It is an impossibility.

Anne Morrow Lindbergh

When you were growing up, maybe you felt like no one wanted to hear from you. You felt that your needs, creativity or exuberance were irritating, annoying to those around you.

Maybe you're currently in a relationship in which you feel cautious about initiating sex or rearranging the furniture, or—more importantly—bringing up your partner's upsetting behaviors.

The fact is, no one can read your mind. Love requires that both people speak up, express themselves, give their input and negotiate how they want to continue to live together. Your partner can't deal with what you don't reveal.

If you are dating, you're laying down the blueprint for how the relationship will be in the future. Don't paint yourself into the background. If you've already done that, grab the vocal and physical expressions of bright red, green and blue paints and start redoing the place called "your relationship." Express yourself—more—today.

I will tell my partner who I am.

❧

If you asked me what I came into this world to do,
I will tell you: I came to live out loud.

Émile Zola

"Two shall be as one" is a common wedding phrase. But it is only possible as a perspective in spiritual consciousness. As unique, embodied individuals, each of us has some interests and behaviors that are nonnegotiable. Consequently, we don't want to live "as one" with our spouse. We want to maintain some aspects of our own specific identity. At the same time we want to be wedded in passionate harmony.

Too often love and harmony get blocked when nonnegotiable characteristics are the object of contempt. Women's gabfests with friends and men's "Monday Night Football" are common activities precious to the ones involved, threats to the spouses. Yet, we need to honor our own nonnegotiable values and interests as well as those of our spouse.

Pick one nonnegotiable activity, interest or behavior of your spouse that you find difficult to understand and/or accept. For today, focus only on your acceptance. See how you can open your heart and mind to see your spouse's way as important, despite your own annoyance or discomfort.

I respect that some differences are nonnegotiable.

∽

Love is the ability to honor and respect the nonnegotiable needs of the other while still honoring the nonnegotiable needs of yourself.

Elizabeth Edson Davis

The most important magic you can make together is the celebration of the ways you are different from each other. The ways you're alike feel comfy and cozy and provide a kind of emotional glue. But the ways that you're different create the excitement, the inspiration to co-create the future together.

Your differences will bring forth challenges, the misunderstandings, the conflicts and the fights. But with a simple change in vision those very same differences become the doorway to your spiritual expansion, learning and growth. Why? Because in order to create lasting love you have to see each other for who you are. Without the differences you would never be you, and you'd never get to experience the magic of being loved for who you truly are—and love your partner in the same way.

How you envision differences will either make or break your marriage. Choose to learn from them, choose to continually find the magic!

I can discover the magic at the heart of our differences.

The meeting of two personalities is like the contact of two chemical substances: if there is any reaction, they are transformed.

Carl Jung

The myth of the perfect "love match" has permeated romantic thinking for generations. It is not only misleading, it is false. There is no such thing. It is only an illusion, an illusion that sends many of us into depression, divorce court and despair.

Great "love matches" happen in novels and especially romance novels. Real men and women are far more complex and far more intricate; they do not lend themselves to flawless illusions of effortless, trouble-free love. When we abandon the seductive forces of illusion, we are finally and for the first time available for real life love. As long as illusion haunts the hallways of our hearts, all we can do is condemn reality to the status of an unfavorable stand-in for what we imagine should be our rightful gift from "Cupid."

Today, keep your focus on what is. Stay conscious to catch those "might have beens" or "should haves" that want to distract you into illusion and corrupt your availability for expressing and receiving real love and affection.

I forgo living in illusion.

Love matches, as they are called, have illusion for their father and need for their mother.

Friedrich Nietzsche

L ife can be very hectic. There's your career, your love life and just everyday requirements. Add to that a child or two (if that's your choice) and the daily demands can feel overwhelming. Too often we lose ourselves, barely remembering that we count also. Love and intimacy deteriorate when we ignore our own physical, emotional and spiritual needs.

It's important that you set aside some time, preferably each day, just to be with yourself, so that you can listen to your own inner wisdom, your own personal connection with God or the Universe. Perhaps you'll notice that you want and need to spend more time with your spouse. Perhaps you'll slip into a state of grace, a gratitude for just being alive.

Set aside a few minutes to be present with yourself. Take the time just to open to yourself, so that when you are with your lover, you've enjoyed a moment of true rest and can open more fully to what you share together.

I will take time for myself.

❧

It is far easier for the Spirit
of God to hit a target that is not moving.
Don't just do something, sit there.

Dale A. Meyer

Maybe liking your spouse doesn't sound very romantic, very sexy. But what about the everyday real romance of just enjoying each other's company? Or is it only soft candlelight and smooth jazz that counts as romance? If so, try expanding romance to include activities, experiences and feelings you'd enjoy with a friend—only they're happening with your lover.

All you have to do is stay conscious of liking your spouse's company. Whether it be shopping together, juggling the travel bags together, even just taking a walk together—if you like being with each other—that can be romance, too! Isn't it a miracle to love the everyday company of the person you enjoy making love with?!

Today, make a list of all the things you like about your spouse, stuff you'd like even if you weren't in love and married. When you're together, even running errands, stay focused on liking your spouse and see if it doesn't make even the errands a romantic event.

I like as well as love my spouse.

*It's an extra dividend when you like
the girl you're in love with.*

Clark Gable

When you make a mistake—get caught rolling your eyes at your spouse, or being overly friendly with someone else at a party—how well are you able to laugh at your own foibles, your own bad behavior? Or do you get defensive and try to claim innocence? Most of us enter marriage on the defensive side, taking ourselves very seriously when we're caught in the wrong.

When you see how ridiculous it is to defend your bad behavior, you can begin to give it up. You see how silly you're being—and you learn to laugh at yourself. That's maturity! Now, when your spouse calls you on some insensitivity or forgetfulness, you don't have to claim innocence. Instead, you can own up and then laugh at yourself. Maybe even laugh together.

The freedom to laugh at yourself releases you to see other people's foibles with compassion and allows you to stay better connected with your spouse when your behavior is less than wonderful.

I can learn to laugh at myself.

❧

You grow up the day you have your first laugh
—at yourself.

Ethel Barrymore

"If it takes effort, it can't be love." "If I have to work at it, that's the end of romance." "If I have to ask, it ruins it." Words from the uninitiated.

Lovework is spiritually necessary to fit two distinctive lives together in romance and conflict, passion and housework. Without lovework there can be no long-lasting love. Real life love requires attention to one another's needs, negotiating conflicts to benefit you both, consciously receiving and giving love. Great loves are always created from the bold dynamics of two distinctly different people— and their ability to thrive on passionate lovework.

Embrace the effort it takes to learn about each other, the time it takes to resolve your differences, the tenderness it takes to find your own sexual freedom and the heartfelt commitment that closed the exit door forevermore. With your care for one another and your willingness to engage in lovework, you'll find your way into a future far more meaningful, more spiritually fulfilling than anything you've ever imagined.

**I make myself available for the lovework
our relationship requires.**

*We're not each other's types and it wasn't instant chemistry.
From the beginning we knew we had to grow the trust and loving
creativity that we now completely rely on.*

Juliana and Joshua Scott

How silly to waste our lives. We fret about mistakes in the past. Worry about events in the future. Pine over lost opportunities. But what about now? Now—this is your life. Not one second to either side—now is the only moment you can truly be alive.

We're not taught how to be alive and loving in the moment. Quite the contrary. Grab your life and live it to the fullest by encountering the present. Right this minute, what are you feeling? Now. What do you really want to do? Now.

While you may not always be able to do what you want or express what you feel in this or that moment, you can learn to stay alive to your own experience. Instead of living in what might have been or what might happen, open your heart to "This is my life" as often as you can!

I know loving is an encounter in the moment.

Creativity is the encounter of the intensively conscious
human being with his or her world.

Rollo May

Hearts are funny things. They're not like red cutouts in Valentine's Day displays. They're not just the vessels pumping blood, keeping us alive. Nor are they just the fourth chakra in the Eastern energy system. Our hearts express all of the above and much, much more, or less, depending on the emotional scar tissue surrounding our ability to love.

If you are on a spiritual path and/or involved in personal growth, the goal is very much the same—to open your heart—to yourself, to everyone else and to God. When you are openly conscious you begin to see it's all God anyway. So the greatest gift you can give yourself is to advance your capacity to love. Like yeast in bread dough, it's the growth agent par excellence.

Having a change of heart means to see compassion where you used to see blame, sadness instead of shame. Changing your heart changes how you see life. Discover God, heart to heart.

I am changing my heart to love more fully.

The most powerful agent of growth and
transformation is something much more basic than
any technique: a change of heart.

John Welwood

17

There's lots of talk about consciousness, but what is it really? Is it being aware? Is it part of self-discovery? Yes and yes.

Think of consciousness as the time between a stimulus and your response. For example, your spouse offers you constructive criticism. You respond without reflection, without the time in between. It's knee-jerk. You can't process the intent of the criticism because your response originates from your past. You get defensive. Then, if your spouse unconsciously gets hooked by your defensiveness, you're both lost. You're both locked into associations from the past. Neither of you is conscious.

But when you take the time to hear the criticism and pause to determine the motivation, then you can be aware of how you decide how to respond. Maybe you appreciate your spouse trying to be helpful but the comment isn't what you need. You can say that with care and appreciation. Neither of you is lost in the past and both of you feel appreciated. You are both using consciousness to be loving.

I consciously commit to loving my spouse.

Consciousness is moving from being reactive
to being intentional in our lives.

Joyce and Andre Patenaude

Remember "If at first you don't succeed, try, try again"? Maybe it sounded sappy or glib, but it's true. Your determination is a powerful force. When you move into your future with desire fueled by conviction, you open the way to success. That doesn't mean it will occur on first attempt, or even second or third. What it does mean is that with determination, in time you'll find a way to succeed.

So many people give up right away—on their marriage, on a date, on romance after the baby comes. It's such a shame. With more curiosity, patience and the realization that nothing worth having comes fully formed, determination can help you reinvent your life in ways far better than you may even be able to imagine.

What do you want from your marriage—realistically— that you can determine to achieve? How do you have to open more with your partner in order to increase your chances of succeeding? Fire up your imagination and begin today!

My determination is powerful.

This proves that if you put your mind to
something and you keep working and keep doing,
your dream does come true.

Madonna

You've heard it said that you create your life, and that's true. But it's also true that there are larger forces playing in your life, directing chance meetings, offering opportunities. Perhaps you've been afraid to break out of certain patterns, afraid to play with Lady Luck, afraid to reap more of the gifts of love.

What would happen if you understood that luck in love is simply the willingness to more fully open the door of your heart to life's invitations—to more readily take a chance, play with life and win?

You can start today, allowing the winds of luck to blow more freely through your heart. First, take a moment to acknowledge someone or something important, who would not be in your life without some luck. Then, open your availability to be visited by luck—some offbeat opportunity, which may be very subtle or small, that could expand the love in your life. With appreciation, go for it!

I consciously notice how lucky I am.

Every day, I think of all the reasons why
I'm lucky to have my wife.

Paul Gonzalez

U nderneath what you choose to show of yourself to the outside world there lives a very fragile "inner child." This inner child still needs comforting because it carries the faded dreams and painful wounds from your early past. This fragile, vulnerable core is alive in both men and women. Share it only in the presence of love you can trust.

When you open to one another seeking comfort, the opening and sharing as well as the comfort create a well-spring of intensely delicious and healing intimacy. Notice that comfort comes in many forms. It may take tender listening, or physical holding, or words of love, support and renewed commitment. Some people may want to play and frolic, others may be in the mood to make love. Comfort is a balm that can open us to new love.

Reveal a sensitive issue to your spouse and ask for comfort. Or perhaps all you can do today is notice what needs comforting.

I'm aware we both need comfort.

Let me enfold thee and hold thee to my heart.

Shakespeare, *Macbeth*

How do you know you're really loved? It's very simple, actually. Are you enjoyed and appreciated for the ways you're different from your spouse? If you know you are valued for who you know yourself to be, not what you do just to please your honey, then you can count on the love being for you.

If you are only "loved" for the ways you're just like your spouse, or the ways your spouse thinks you "should" be—that's not love. That's just you catering to someone who is self-centered.

At the heart of love is the ability to discover and enjoy one another for your differences. It's the differences that keep love always fresh and changing. Today, express how much you cherish your spouse's traits and endearments, especially those that are different from yours. Ask your spouse to tell you what about you is most appealing and most endearing.

Our differences are at the heart of love.

*I believe that basically people are people ...
but it is our differences which charm,
delight and frighten us.*

Agnes Newton Keith

If you are dating, there's a sure-fire way to protect yourself from chasing unavailable "future heartbreaks." Be yourself at all times. That way, no matter what happens, your date will stick around only if he's interested, only if she finds who you are to be really attractive. This advice also holds if you're not sure about the future of your current relationship. Check out reality. Just be yourself and watch the response.

Sound too easy? Well, it's not easy for most people, but it's very simple. There's no game playing, no trying to "catch" someone. It's just straight up getting to know each other. If you like each other—great! If you don't, what a success! You've saved yourself a lot of wasted time. Afraid the other person might not like you as is? That's understandable. But what do you gain by wearing a mask, putting on a show and never knowing where you stand?

Date as though the life of your soul depended on it. It does!

I will be true to myself right from the start.

❧

*The emotional tragedy of heartbreak
can be avoided if honesty is present right
from the beginning.*

Grace Cornish

"**Y**ou don't care!" "You're so caught up in yourself!" "You ask how I am, but you don't really listen!" Sound familiar? Sadly, so many couples cheat their relationship by avoiding the deep intimacy of sincere interest in each other's lives, moods and desires. It's as if romance, laughter and fun were the only experiences worth showing up for. Not so.

The more you can open your heart and mind to learn about your partner, to learn about who he is beneath the surface, how she experiences the world, the more of a connection and private bond you can share with each other. That is a kind of real romance that cannot be found on the beaches of Tahiti. It can't even be found in a good roll in the hay. It's only available by opening to each other, in the presence of genuine, loving interest.

Stretch your focus out beyond your own day's events, with a wide-reaching interest in your spouse. Ask questions to help you learn more. Increase your interest!

**Genuine interest is one of the best gifts
I can give my love.**

*The more you try to be interested in other people,
the more you find out about yourself.*

Thea Astley

It can be very romantic to write love notes or poetry to your spouse. Maybe you don't think you're much of a writer. But you don't have to be a great writer to put your feelings on paper and create a surprise. You can express sentiments you're too shy to say in person. Or maybe you need to apologize or ask forgiveness. You can use note writing just for special occasions or anytime you want to express your love.

Write funny, sweet or tender notes and sneak them into your spouse's purse, briefcase or lunch box or tape them to a mirror, stove top or car windshield—to be found later! You can even use cartoons. Your honey will love you for being so creative and fun. The two of you may even want to save your notes in a memory album.

Love notes help develop your special connection. You can be as creative and boldly intimate as you want. Start today!

I will write love notes to my sweetheart.

I had written a poem for her.
I put it on thick paper then stained it with coffee and burned it all
around the edges
So it looked like an old scroll.

Rob Hann

It's important to have an idea of what you want from life, from your marriage, from love. At the same time, it's just as important to realize that you can't control the outcome, can't choreograph the way it will look and feel. So, it's necessary to hope and to desire—and, at the same time, to surrender to life on life's terms. That's mature hope.

Most people miss out on life's bounty by insisting too specifically on what's "supposed" to happen. In fact, you can kill the pleasure of life with immature hope that can't be satisfied with anything else but only and exactly what is hoped for.

Give your hope the best possible chance. Consciously hope with all your heart and soul for something special in your love life—then set it free. Be open to the possibility that it will come true and welcome that possibility. At the same time stay aware that it may not occur and that you can find your pleasure in other ways.

I will hope with surrender.

I was thirty-five years old. I hadn't given up hope
that I would meet the man of my dreams, but
I was open to the fact that I might not.

Michelle Pfeiffer

Your partner is not you. Sounds simple enough, right? Yet, most marriages end because of the refusal to share two realities. When you really understand that the other is not you, you'll learn to see your spouse's ideas, feelings and behaviors as just as valid and important for her as yours are for you. You grasp that he's not being resistant when he disagrees with you. You'll be able to embrace the exquisitely exciting distance between the two of you—rather than trying to squash you both into the same mold.

Not until you grasp that the other is not you can you experience the new intimacy in which you get to be loved for who you really are and love your partner in the same way.

Today, practice seeing everyone you encounter as "not me." Rather than judge their different ways, practice opening your curiosity. Wonder how they see the world, differently from the way you do. Notice how your perspective on all of life is enlarged.

I know my partner is not me.

What made it work was understanding—by both of us — that there were two people in the relationship.

Jeanne Moutousammy Ashe
(widow of Arthur Ashe)

Here's a way of experiencing just how your partner is not you. In matters of conflict in a marriage there is never the truth. It is folly to think you have the truth and your spouse has none. You can certainly know more about a topic than your spouse, but marital conflicts are never about knowledge. They're always the clash between two different ways of seeing and experiencing something.

If you want to find your truths, open yourselves to dimensions of awareness beyond the obvious. Look for motivations in each of your early childhood experiences. How are each of you duplicating your parents' not-so-great behaviors? There's always more than meets the eye when you go looking for each of your truths.

By all means, put forward both of your points of view. Then sample the wisdom in one another's position. Somewhere between the two of you there is much to learn. Work together to find it. Beware claiming yours as the only truth.

I agree that both of us have a piece of the truth.

❧

Whoever undertakes to set himself up as a
judge in the field of truth and knowledge is shipwrecked
by the laughter of the gods.

Albert Einstein

We all know the phrase—"lovers' quarrels." They come with the territory. In fact, if you never quarrel, if you never get angry, never fight—you are emotionally cheating on your relationship. Why? Because, no matter how terrific you both may be, you are still going to get on each other's nerves. You are going to disagree on the "right" way to carve the turkey, negotiate a raise, drive to Texas.

You're going to tease each other about your particular idiosyncrasies, and someone's going to get their feelings hurt. Someone's going to misunderstand the grocery list and come home without the most necessary item for the company coming to dinner. Someone's going to spoil the vacation by drinking the water, even after they were warned. Love happens while you're living your ordinary life—and stuff happens that's really annoying!

By all means—quarrel. Just remember that it's part of making love, not war. You're just working out the emotional gunk that builds up—that's all.

I care enough to quarrel.

The quarrels of lovers are the renewal of love.

Horace

Without attention to romance, it will die. It needs planning and emotional availability. It thrives on your creativity and pleasure. It fades away when ignored or manipulated.

No matter how long you've been together, it's never too late to put more romance back into your love. Surprise one another with flowers. And don't just drop them on the table. Make sure you present them as a romantic love gift. Make special dates just for romance, either at home or at a hotel. (While these evenings may lead to sex, that's not the point.) The point is to experience anything and everything that the two of you find romantic.

For dinner at home: a gorgeous table set with candles and beautiful flowers, cool jazz and fine wine to set off a sumptuous meal. Flirt with each other, as if it were a first date. Dance to your favorite love songs. Take turns reading romantic and/or erotic poetry. Remind yourselves why it was the wisest choice you've ever made to marry each other.

I joyfully open to more romance.

After twenty-two years of marriage,
we still keep our romance alive, by having special
romantic dinners and evenings.

Terry and Evey Sherven

M ost suffering is caused by the refusal to live in reality. How do we do this? We develop an idea of how love is supposed to be and we marry it instead of our flesh-and-blood spouse. Then when reality is different from what it's "supposed to be," we're devastated. We rail at God, we blame our spouse, we suffer the torture of the damned.

When you accept reality, you can embrace the vast expanse of experiences and emotions that come to you. From a spiritual perspective, your soul needs these experiences to show you who you really are. From a romantic perspective, love gets richer the more you live in reality.

Yes, bad things happen. But when you accept life on life's terms, you open yourself to grief, to anger, to needing one another, to love. Always, always, there is a way to see love in almost any experience if you will but keep your heart open to reality. Open to love the beauty of reality!

I see the blessings in all realities.

When we stop running away, when we really accept,
that is when even tragedy succumbs to beauty.

Katherine Mansfield

In an effort to be pleasing, most people make happiness very difficult, if not impossible. Allergic to confrontation and the conflict of differences, many people wait for the other person to make all the decisions—only to end up feeling resentful and disappointed.

One of the greatest gifts you can give your partner is to be decisive and make it clear where you stand. Whether it's where you'd like to go on vacation or what color sheets you want, there are very few "unimportant issues." That's because you are building a life together and to do that takes input from both of you.

Making decisions is a skill that is learned. If you aren't good at it, you need to practice—every day. Realize that you can change your mind, or do it differently next time. Focus on being clear where you stand on every issue that comes up today.

Real love requires that I be decisive.

❧

All the great decisions in my life have been made in less than half an hour.

Carmen Maura

Mornings can be brutal. Lots of people wait until the very last minute to get up and then rush around like maniacs getting themselves (and kids) ready for the day. There's no time to feel connected, much less romantic, with each other.

Yet, mornings are a perfect time to connect and start the day with love. What could be better?! And it just takes making connection a priority. Start by giving yourself plenty of time, even if you need to go to bed a half hour earlier. You'll like the benefits of a little loving in the morning.

Start your romantic mornings by setting the alarm for five to fifteen minutes before you have to get up, and just snuggle. Then, even if you have kids, develop a getting-ready routine that involves all of you helping to celebrate the love you all share. Don't forget to say "I love you" in your private way before you go off to the rest of your day. That's a Good Morning!

I will make our morning time romantic.

We get to share the morning together
in a peaceful and relaxing way, which sets the
tone for the rest of the day.

Karsten Hojberg

February

*The world is full of currents
we can't lay corporeal hands on—
trust, faith, gravity, magnetic fields,
love. . . . They add richness
to all our hours.*

ERMA J. FISK

We live in a society obsessed with having "fun." Generally that means distracting ourselves from life, from relationships. We're addicted to watching meaningless TV, partying, being otherwise unconscious and out of touch with ourselves and each other. And we call that "fun." No wonder so many people are depressed, caught up in chemical addictions, wondering what they're missing.

Real fun occurs when you are living your passion. When you find work you love. When you contribute to society in some way that expresses your joy, your concerns, your talents.

Real fun comes with using yourself, not avoiding yourself. Real fun in your marriage can mean fulfilling your passion together.

What do you and your spouse really care about? What can you do that would be deeply satisfying and expand the joy and meaning of being together—as well as benefit society? Today, commit yourself to having more real fun in your life and in your love.

Following my passion is fun.

☙

I believe that God put us here to have fun. Which doesn't mean going to discos. It means leading a fulfilled life.

Max Kennedy

Each of us has the God-given power to choose how we live our lives. Yes, we may have entered life handicapped by family limitations or financial pressures. But God's abundance is always waiting for you—you just have to turn in your meal ticket. The question is—are you ready to eat filet mignon?

God gave us the powers of thought and imagination. With these capabilities we were given the power to create our lives. Too often the blueprint we develop leaves out Divine Intervention, the Chance Encounter, the Miracle. Then when God's Room Service shows up, our minds go blank, our eyes go blind. The opportunity for abundance disappears.

Allow God to dance in your love. Stay open to magical moments, unusual occurrences, the flight of fancy that gives your love a larger range. In your imagination, picture a dining table where God's Room Service has delivered a feast that honors the two of you and all the abundance you can be. Eat! Enjoy! Be it!

I trust God's abundance and welcome it.

I look at my life and know some presence or power has had a hand in it. If you just allow that hand to guide you, you'll be fine.

Ving Rhames

Power is such a scary idea for so many people, as if it only means power over others. But that's never real power. That's oppression and domination. In your relationship, how have you been trying to control things, attempting to have power over your partner? Even in just little ways?

Personal power is the power of the self. It is self-respect and self-responsibility, enabling you to stand separate from your spouse and others and express your truth while respecting your spouse and others for their truth. Personal power directs you to lead your life with vitality and boldness. It enables you to follow your passion. It loves through you wisely and well.

Whatever sets your heart and soul on fire is your passion. What do you need to do to have this passion expressed in your life, in your marriage? Do it! Because personal power is the soul on fire.

**Personal power is God-given and
mine to use wisely.**

*For God hath not given us the spirit of fear; but of power,
and of love, and of a sound mind.*

2 Timothy 1:7

Love embraces idiosyncrasies, cares for hurts and is compassionate in its criticism. Yet, so many of us imagine that once we're settled in with someone it's our job to find fault, to fix him, to make her over—as if that's what love is. But it's not.

Finding fault is an expression of fear: fear of our spouse's ways that are different from our own, or different from how we are certain "things should be." We're shut down to reality being any other way than our own. Think about it. When we're not fearful, we don't want to find fault. Then, out of love, we may offer constructive criticism—not attacking or disempowering, but based in a genuine concern for the other person's well-being. Fault finding is heartless and only concerned with comforting our own insecurity.

Today, be aware of what your fears are when you want to find fault. That is the best way for you to seek the comfort you hope for.

Today I offer constructive criticism.

⁂

Faults are thick where love is thin.

English Proverb

Did you have fantasies that when you fell in love everything in your life would suddenly be taken care of? You'd feel complete, redeemed from all the insecurity and pain that burdened your life?

Most of us have had those wishes. But it simply isn't possible. Love is not a quick fix for anything. In fact, the presence of real love can often expose even more self-doubt and uncertainty than when you are alone. That's part of love's job—to put us in touch with self-sabotaging feelings that prevent us from being loved more fully. That way, our wounds can be loved and we can be healed by our intimate relationships.

Don't expect to be saved by love. Do expect to face experiences that invite you to open up, to face yourself more fully, to come to know your spouse more deeply. Today, look past the fantasy of the Band-Aid and open to the richness of all the experience real love actually offers.

Our love is not a Band-Aid.

❧

Being in love with someone and being with someone is work,
and it's daily, and it's not a Band-Aid.

Whoopi Goldberg

Do you get caught up trying to outdo yourself, year after year—for her birthday present, his anniversary present? Do you think you have to spend a lot of money in order to convey the depth of your love?

First of all, unless you have unlimited resources, help yourselves by putting a limit on what you're going to spend on one another (and for your kids) for gifts. That, in itself, will be a gift of relaxation and clarity to you both and to your savings account. Now focus on what you want your gifts to express. Great gifts say, "I see you and want you to be happy." So all year long, pick up clues about what activities, entertainment, relaxation and other stuff would really touch a special chord. Don't forget to express your love throughout the year with little, whimsical gifts.

Give of yourself—be creative. When you select a gift, feel your love reflected in the choice. Enjoy the giving!

I give my lover gifts with heart.

And remember, the very best gifts
come from the heart.

Kinsley Foster

Why do people put up with relationships in which they are plagued with fears that they cannot trust their husband or wife? The answer is simple, really. These people are not trustworthy themselves. They failed to seriously check out the other person's reliability, integrity and honesty in the beginning, before they were ever married. Yet, they want to blame their partner for any betrayal they may experience.

In order to enjoy the pleasure of deep trust in your relationship, you must be trustworthy yourself, able to risk penetrating explorations of your loved one's motives, truth-telling and genuine love for you.

Today, ask a question of your partner that you've been afraid to ask. Just by asking, you become more trustworthy. Now listen carefully to not just the answer you get—listen also to how your spouse answers. Is it with care for your concerns, or with gruff irritation? Is it with a desire to have you know more, or with jealous privacy? Your asking and attention to the response you get will allow you to trust yourself more, and hopefully your lover as well.

I will be more trustworthy.

✤

Without trust, words become the hollow sound of a wooden gong.
With trust, words become life itself.

John Harold

The tomorrow you imagine is coming will never come. Tomorrow will show up on its own terms. So the only time that you have for certain, on your terms, is right now. The most important question you can ask is: What do I want to do?

What do you want to do? Allow the question to permeate your life and set your soul on fire. You may not be able to live some of the answers yet. Lack of money or courage may limit you. But while the question keeps igniting your spirit, notice how you are shown new pathways to change your life. Notice that your desire can overtake fear.

Live fiercely inside your desire, inside your answer. Love yourself with a passion that drives you to express that answer—with your life. Do what you can today. Even if it's just a phone call to begin to get information. That phone call is an expression of love for yourself. Keep calling.

**I love fiercely today,
tomorrow might not come.**

*You don't know what's going to happen.
You need to do whatever you want to do today,
because tomorrow might not come.*

Jennifer Lopez

Sometimes spur of the moment plans are great fun. But what about the thrill and excitement of anticipation? Planning ahead, looking forward to a special time together—that kind of expectation is also very romantic.

How often do you extend invitations for Love-Play dates—not necessarily for sex, but just for special times together? Do you wait, hoping your spouse will cook something up? Aw, come on. The more you invite, the more your spouse will come out to play. Get creative. A note on a newspaper travel photo saying, "Wow! Am I looking forward to this weekend with you!" so she knows what to expect. A massage area set up in a garden or your bedroom so he knows what's happening after work. A restaurant card marked "You and Me—7 P.M."

Intrigue. Having to wait. Knowing you'll soon be enjoying each other. Start today. Leave a message on your lover's e-mail or voicemail with a Love-Play invitation for tonight.

I accept my spouse's love-play invitations.

With notes and stuff we make invitations to
one another for later fun and games.

Barbara Steffin and Nick Rath

Y̵ou put one foot in front of the other to walk, right? You brush your teeth every morning, and go through the same motions to do your hair, makeup or shave, right? You don't even think about it. But that wasn't the case when you first mastered these skills. Then you had to practice over and over until they were part of you.

Well, now it's time to make love a daily habit. While this may sound mechanical or forced, it's merely the awareness and actions necessary to make love with each other throughout the day.

So, how can you make loving part of your morning "drill"? Snuggling in bed, making each other coffee, wishing one another success at work, a kiss and "I love you" before going your separate ways. What else? And throughout the day? There's e-mail notes, phone calls, each other's photo on your desk or vehicle visor, lunch dates. What works for you? In the evening? Be creative—and make love a fun habit!

I make loving a daily habit.

Love is a product of habit.

Lucretius

Maybe your vacation is coming or you're about to celebrate your birthday. You know just how it's going to be. You're soooooo excited! But then it doesn't go at all like you expected. Not remotely! You're devastated. You blame your lover for wrecking everything. He should have known! She should have understood. Why is life so awful?

Well, life can dish out some pretty painful experiences, but devastated expectations shouldn't be one of them. We do that dirty little trick to ourselves. We decide that we're God, and that we know exactly how "it should be" and then when our lover does it differently, or life has other plans for us, we can't stay open to reality, to the mystery of being alive. We pout, sulk and blame everyone but ourselves for our suffering.

Beware of your rigid expectations. Today, practice living in the unknown, available to experience that actually happens instead of insisting that life only go your way. Enjoy the discovery!

I let go of expectations.

❧

When your illusions clash with reality,
when your falsehoods clash with truth,
then you have suffering.

Anthony deMello

"I thought I'd died and gone to heaven" is a phrase that attempts to speak for the rapture, the ecstasy available to us anytime we're willing to surrender, to be surprised by love's heat, to be stirred by what we find inside when we're melted by love. To become available for these spiritually transcendent moments, we must give up control, discard rigid expectations and trust that God intended us to be in the Oneness—at least from time to time.

So often we block love's power, thinking we know how it "should" be. But love knows better. As we trust ourselves to care more deeply for our spouse, and receive the miracle of being loved for all that we are—limitations, brilliance, everything—only then can we move into the sacred transcendence of ecstasy. It doesn't happen overnight or all the time—and it takes practice.

Today, love with all your heart and soul, knowing there's still more heaven to come as you increasingly open to the intimate spirituality of ecstasy.

I am open to experience ecstasy.

The soul should always stand ajar, ready to welcome the ecstatic experience.

Emily Dickinson

How often do you express your love to your partner, and have it ignored, rebuffed or corrected? Feels terrible, doesn't it? Why does this happen between people who love each other? Because each of you harbors certain ideas of what love looks like and feels like, and you wear blinders to other ways of loving. Silly, isn't it?

The art of receiving love requires opening to the mystery of love—taking off the restrictions to its expression—and making yourself available for any form it may want to take with you. Your spouse wasn't put on Earth to love you just the way you say so. Your spouse loves you in his or her own way. It's your responsibility to greet love however it comes to call, grateful for the gifts it chooses to leave with you.

Learn from each other how you express love. It can even be while washing the dishes. It's like that. Mysterious and delicious. Daily. Daily.

I receive love in all its expressions.

It seems to me that we often, almost sulkily,
reject the good that God offers us because, at the moment,
we expected some other good.

C. S. Lewis

Valentine's Day can be very commercial and materialistic. It can feel like a day of obligation rather than celebration. So make sure you personalize how the two of you will thank Cupid for bringing you together.

Celebrating your love doesn't even need to cost you much. You can get some three-by-five cards and some of those stickers (with hearts, roses and anything else that's meaningful) at the stationery store and then create several different cards that you can leave around the house in special places to be discovered throughout the day. You can make her favorite dessert and decorate it with white, red and pink—whipped cream, roses and little heart candies.

Whatever you do, make sure you are honoring the two of you, and your very specific relationship. Don't just go buy flowers and candy. Put your heart and soul and creativity into it—that's what makes it fun for you both. Happy Valentine's Day!

**I will do something really creative
to celebrate my valentine.**

*On Valentine's Day, my son and his friends prepared
dinner for their girlfriends. The women were overwhelmed
by their actions. Each one had a rose on her plate and
a heart balloon tied to the back of her chair.*

Karla Kelly

Are you constantly comparing your relationship with the couple down the block or some celebrity's marriage? Do you suffer heartbreak because you don't have what they have? Do you read romance novels, aching for that kind of swept-away dream? Or do you have your feet planted squarely in reality, grateful for the real romance you've created with the loving partner who shares your heart and your bed?

If you're wasting your life pining for what you don't have, please be suspicious of your investment in suffering, in melodrama, rather than loving and being loved. You are living your priorities. If you choose to pine, ask yourself, "What do I achieve by insisting on suffering?" Don't allow yourself the cop-out of, "I don't know." Have you always gone without, and it feels normal? Do you get lots of attention for your suffering? Look deep inside.

Today, allow yourself to focus only on the value of what you have. Banish pining at least for today.

I desire only what's possible.

*I've never let myself get into a situation of pining away
for someone or something I couldn't have.*

Jamie Lee Curtis

To listen, heart and soul, is to love. To listen to each new day is to open to the divine. No day has ever been the same, ever, throughout the history of the universe. Stand in awe. Wonder at the beauty and the majesty that each day brings.

No matter what happened yesterday between you and your beloved, today is a new day. It is not a time to hold a grudge or expect the miracle of yesterday's passion to duplicate itself. It is a time unto itself. What will you listen for? What will you open to? If you quiet the rumblings in your mind, you can hear your soul calling to you, beckoning you to open to new love, to open in a way that was unknown only yesterday—but today it is a miracle.

Each day has its own rhythm, its own energy, its own message. Each day reaches down into your soul and asks that you die to yesterday, to be reborn in new love.

Each new day, I learn more about love.

❧

Each day comes with its own song,
a song that no one has ever
seen or heard before.

David Rothenberg

Many times when rage hides in frozen silence or erupts in searing blasts, the desire to punish rushes forward, seducing love with righteousness. We've all felt it, that mind-bending certainty that our lover deserves to be punished for the pain they just caused us. As if we'd never done anything hurtful. As if they'd lived a life of ease and splendor, and now it's their turn to suffer.

The desire to punish is pure animal instinct. It is not an impulse born of consciousness and compassion. For if compassion were in charge, we would never want our beloved to suffer, even if they'd hurt us. We would know that they had already suffered mightily in this life, and that their hurtful behavior was probably some remnant of that suffering.

We all need to learn to be more conscious, more sensitive. None of us needs to be punished. Punishment only begets more punitive behavior. Ask for change, suggest new behavior, teach by example. Never punish love.

I relinquish any need to punish anyone.

If we could read the secret history of those
we would like to punish, we would find in each life
enough grief and suffering to make us stop
wishing anything more on them.

Source Unknown

Personal relationships are the blueprint for all other aspects of society. Primitive consciousness teaches us to put ourselves before others—the survival of the fittest. It's based on a concern for lack, for mere survival. This kind of retrograde thinking still dominates much of the world. Civil wars, starvation and international strife are the proof of it.

You are not powerless. How you relate to those around you—all of those around you—influences every single person you encounter—for good or for not. As you open your heart more fully to your lover, take this new openness into your work world, into the stores where you shop and certainly into your relationships with children and friends.

Be a model for love and respect for others, a model for fairness and equity. Be a model for love, that others can practice what they see you doing and being. Your love has power—use it lavishly.

As I change, I help society change.

※

Personal change is inseparable from
social and political change. Intimate relationships
cannot flourish under conditions of
inequality and unfairness.

Harriet Lerner

You may know that building a muscle requires stressing that muscle through exercise, and the growth occurs in the healing. Well, you are no different. In order to grow spiritually and personally, to become stronger, you have to be stretched. In order to let your brilliance shine, you have to be healed of old, disempowering wounds. The trials of romantic love are the perfect workout lab for that transformational process.

The friction of your differences is God's gift to your soul work. You don't have to pay anyone to create it or supply equipment for it. The friction comes with any intense romance, once the honeymoon phase is over.

Now, in order to learn to love through and through, the natural conflicts of intimacy will expose your self-centered impulses, defensive instincts and the desire to hurt back when you've been hurt. Those arise from old wounds that need healing. As you go through this alchemical process, the diamond that you are will be cut, honed, buffed and polished to its brilliance.

I become my best through adversity.

❧

The diamond cannot be polished without friction,
nor the man perfected without trials.

Chinese Proverb

"We need to talk" sounds like a doctor getting ready to give you a diagnosis of cancer. Yet, this is one of the most common introductions to intimate matrimonial conversation. Ominous. Unnerving. Scary!

The problem results from our fear of confrontation and anxiety when asking for change. Love isn't the guiding experience. Fear rules. So these conversations are hateful, loveless panderings to obligation rather than an intimate exchange and negotiation of desires.

Communication is always an exchange of desires, even if all you desire is to be heard telling a story or a joke. So, when you can embrace your lover's desire—as just as legitimate and valuable as your own—then any conversation is an opportunity to learn about one another and learn from one another. Then, "Let's make a couch date" sounds inviting, a promise of more love to come. Even if you're asked to change, it will be during an open conversation filled with love and desire.

Respectful communication is always a two-way street.

Communication is an exchange of desires.
Surrender your desires to one another and you'll
have honest, intimate communication.

Melody Starr

Many people hold back on love—to be safe. As if they would die if they experienced the new intimacy. Yes, if their old identity died, that would bring about new life. It would be unfamiliar. Might be dangerous. They could get hurt.

Here's the deal. You either hide from love and play it safe, or you risk and open your heart to love. If you open yourself, know you will definitely get hurt. But you won't die and won't suffer for long, unless you imagine it should be safe all the time. You simply can't love without getting hurt.

We were made to love, not to play it safe. We were made to love, get hurt by the clash of differences, and learn to recover through understanding and forgiveness. We become resilient lovers and learn to love even more fiercely. We were not intended to hide under the covers of fear and loneliness. Come out, play in the sea of love—and ride the waves!

I live to love, not play it safe.

✧

A ship in harbor is safe,
but that is not what ships are built for.

John Shedd

When you agree to play in the sea of love—wading out beyond the safety of what is familiar—you enter the magic of new possibilities. All you have to do is risk yourself.

Love is always the process of risking more of yourself, making yourself more and more available so that someone can enjoy you and love you. It's possible they might not understand you or might even leave you. That's true. But why be with someone you can't trust to embrace you for all that you are? Don't sell yourself short.

Today, take a risk. Reveal something that's important to you. Make a request for change in your relationship. Express a need to be held, made love to, be appreciated for the work you do, or have someone else take care of the kids. Pay a compliment that would reveal your attraction. Take a risk and see what happens.

I risk opening my heart.

Change and growth take place when a
person has risked himself, and dares to become involved
in experimenting with his own life.

Herbert Otto

People are so often shocked when they learn that so-and-so has been having a sexual affair, cheating on the marriage. But they fail to notice that both wife and husband have been cheating—emotionally—for some time before the sexual cheating ever began. There is never an innocent "victim" and a guilty "cheat." Well-nurtured love never invites the outside dalliance.

Love, like orchids, cannot bear to be ignored. The care and feeding of romantic love requires continual lovework—weeding and pruning by negotiating conflicts and hurt feelings, while at the same time continually fertilizing with real romance and deepening intimacy. Holding back, lying, refusing to fight, denying love gifts, giving top loyalty to parents or kids—it's all emotional cheating, which is every bit as damaging as sexual cheating. Sexual cheating is always the by-product of both people's neglect.

Honor love with your full commitment. Give your love what it needs to grow and flourish, and neither of you will be tempted to stray.

I bring myself fully to our love.

Love does not brook neglect.

Menander

In the beginning there was ecstasy. Then there was the shock of reality. Now there is the challenge of your differences. The earlier ecstasy pointed the way to what is possible, but you must live your lives into the miracle of spiritual oneness. You cannot hang on to first bliss and think it is the whole of love. Yet, so many do, constantly trying to get back to the beginning, when that's all it can ever be—the beginning.

Romantic love is so enchanting as the two of you find one another in the fullness of passion's embrace. Never has anyone been so special, so perfect. Created just for you. But it lasts for just a short time. Then the spell is broken. Now your relationship requires conscious participation. Do you care enough to do the lovework that will safely turn your differences into a mosaic—into the magic of differences?

Romantic love enticed you. Real life invites you. The heavens wait for your answer.

Love is a continual journey into grace.

❧

A good marriage is one that can survive the ninety-day euphoria of romantic love.

Edward Abbey

We all know people who are divorced. You may be one yourself. It's possible other people you know will divorce. Understand that all failed relationships result from ignorance about what love is and lack of skills and vision needed to make love last. What can you say? How do you help?

Open your compassion to anyone suffering from relationship failure. But don't allow yourself to be pulled into a pity party. Pity and prolonged suffering can only help create a love victim. They'll learn nothing, then go back into the world and create the same old mess all over again.

Constructive divorce alerts both people that, for the next time, they need to be better prepared. Suggest they read *The New Intimacy: Discovering the Magic at the Heart of Your Differences* to gain a new vision of mature love, the why and how-to for expanding their love skills. They may need counseling. You can help support and love them while they recover and get themselves ready to love again.

I will be supportive of people going through divorce.

∞

I went through a lot of pain in my divorce.
It made me feel empathy for people I don't even like,
because they're going through it.
I grant them all the slack I can.

Bill Murray

Caught up in the challenges of daily life, it's so easy to feel distant from each other. You didn't get that special call during lunch. You couldn't meet at your kid's ball game, where you love to shout and cheer together. It's late when you get home, you're both tired and connecting seems like the last thing you have energy for.

The truth is, despite all the missed opportunities, you've never been separated. You live in each other's minds and hearts. Call upon your deep coupling and, when you do, it will be there. By knowing that your lover dwells in your consciousness, you are connected in soul. Yes, it's important and critical to express that connection through words and actions—but what you have between you need never wither. It is the bridge that spans any distance that arises during your day.

Rely upon it. It is always already there! Trust that connection. Then you will be together—forever everywhere.

I know we're always connected.

⇛

When one tugs at a single thing in nature, he finds it connected to the rest of the universe.

John Muir

Is it difficult for you to see how your childhood can contribute to painful experiences in your marriage? Consciously, you may want to avoid precisely these kinds of hurtful encounters, yet they occur anyway.

Think about this. When you get pushed to the max, how do you act out your frustration and anger? Especially in those instances when your partner suffers in response, how is your behavior similar to the way your parent(s) treated you? Don't brush this idea away. Every one of us took in the ways of our parents—even their worst stuff. So it's no accident when we treat our lovers in the same ways we experienced at the knees of our parents—where would we have learned differently?

The more you don't want to inflict the kind of pain you endured as a child, the more consciously you can stop duplicating the negative ways of your parents. You grow in maturity, love and grace, and then you can forgive your parents for their limitations.

I break my allegiance to parental negativity.

I think most of the ills of our society can be traced to bad parenting or no parenting at all.

Dennis Miller

No one is complete, whole or truly balanced when alone. We are, each of us, emotionally bent in very specific ways by life. We unconsciously seek someone whose differences will balance us, bring us into greater harmony with ourselves and with life.

Sad to say, after the initial honeymoon period wears off, we tend to forget about our need for balance and look upon our lover's ways as "weird," "bad," "unacceptable." We can actually believe that our own bendings are the only way to go. But that's never the case. We all need balance—all of us. And marriage is one of the very best experiences to fulfill that need, when we keep in mind that our spouse's different ways help us do this.

Today, notice how your partner's ways help to balance or offset your own. Notice how they help you live more easily, more fully, more gracefully.

Our differences balance me.

≫

We balance each other. We're compatible
because of our differences.

Trisha Yearwood and Robert Reynolds

For most people, the everyday demands of life can be pretty intense. It may be difficult to connect with each other during the day. Your weekends may be booked up with your children's activities. Many couples get so out of touch with each other that love fades away. So don't forget to take special time to be together every week.

Make a regular weekly date. Depending on your budget, you can make a special dinner at home, go out to a favorite restaurant, or just go to a local café for a cup of coffee and dessert. The point is to be together, to connect over the events of your lives, and even more importantly to make eye contact, to express your loving feelings for each other, to speak of the pleasure of being together.

Don't forget to date, to enjoy each other. Often. Dating is not just for single people, it's any time you can be together, without the kids, and get to know each other more intimately.

I will make sure we have special dates.

Dating can be a wonderful opportunity for
self-discovery and learning more about one another.
Don't just focus on "having fun."

Kyla Edwards

March

*Tell me to what you
pay attention and I will tell
you who you are.*

JOSÉ ORTEGA Y GASSET

It is a wise person who lives as a student of his own life, who creates anew from the lessons of her learning. There is much to be learned even from the surface realities of your relationship. But more important are the meanings beneath the obvious, the mystery awaiting your inquiry.

The events of your relationship are symbolic of deeper meaning. Within that meaning awaits a message about the love you share—or the crying out for need of love. Look to see what the significance is. The deeper purpose is always trying to advance love or it's showing you that intimacy is being held back in some way.

Your inner process is manifested in outer form. Reading your life is the process of studying the signals for what you are to learn next. Always, you can ask, what am I intending to learn from this experience?

I explore the deeper meaning of our relationship.

⊶⊷

Every event has significance, symbolism and meaning.
Look to see where is the love or
where is it lacking.

Corinne McLaughlin and
Gordon Davidson

W hen you feel angry and express it in a direct, respectful and loving way, you are giving the other person one of the most vulnerable parts of yourself. You are announcing that somehow your emotional and/or physical boundaries have been crossed, you are hurt and feel uncared for. Your anger announces your need to be better treated.

Unfortunately, too many of us learned in childhood that it wasn't "nice" to be angry, that you should protect everyone from your displeasure. But when you ignore your anger, you vote to disempower yourself and you turn yourself into a doormat for everyone else to walk on.

Your anger is a sacred gift from the Creator. It signals that you feel violated. It is frequently your best resource for getting someone's attention and getting a new understanding of what you need. Today, pay attention to your anger. It may be about past issues from childhood, it may apply to changes needed in your current relationship. Today, just notice your anger.

I value my anger as a gift.

❧

Anger is a reminder of our openness and tender heart.
We could not get so enraged with those we love
unless we felt this larger vulnerability with them.

John Welwood

If you refuse to change, you refuse the gift of life. It's as simple as that! From the miracle of conception, you've been changing. Your brain developed in response to changes in your environment. You advanced through school by constantly changing your ability to learn. Yet, when it comes to romantic love, so many people refuse change, refuse to become more, refuse to be touched by God's full spectrum of experience.

Change is the lifeblood of romance and meaningful intimacy. It signifies your willingness to be transformed by love, your openness to allowing love to work its wonders on you. If you won't change, you try to grab onto love and make it do your bidding—that's always a disaster. So, don't do it.

Keep your life and your marriage alive and growing. Keep yourself continually fascinating to your spouse. Surprise even yourself. Actively change your routines, meet new people, play with your spouse. Make change part of your everyday diet. Be open! Be inventive! Have fun!

I welcome change.

≫

Change is so important. Otherwise it's so easy to get stuck.
When you're always changing it's refreshing for you—
and it's refreshing for your relationship.

Patti Hansen

You're going along, things are pretty good. All of a sudden an unexpected opportunity to have more love and abundance presents itself. And you pass on by. In some way, you say "No." Why would you do such a thing? Because you were just going along, life was pretty good, and that was how it was going to be.

We've all done it—short-circuited God's attempts to help us reach a larger state of being. Blocked the possibility of more rich blessings being presented to us. Why? Because we didn't know better. Because we learned to resign ourselves to life "as is." Because change seemed too scary.

Well, it's time to prepare yourself for all the opportunities that want to come to you, if you'll just make yourself ready. All you have to do is open your imagination to become available for the small and large miracles you seek out. Embrace them, especially those that come through your lover. And let them prepare you for even more.

I prepare for more love in my life.

≫

*You have to do things to prepare for
when opportunities come.*

Calista Flockhart

To be good friends with your spouse means to have one another's best interests at heart. That can lead to challenging each other to give up old, outmoded ways. It can be the rich banter and loving competition that spurs you to be your very best at whatever is important. It can push you to take risks you never thought possible. You can be wonderful teachers and coaches for each other, and, at the same time, safe and trusting students.

It's so easy to get defensive when your spouse challenges how you do things. But what are you really defending? Why waste the opportunity to learn more about yourself and a quality of loving that happens only within deep friendship?

Welcome the challenges you present to each other. Let them be your teachers and guides.

I enjoy how we challenge each other.

We challenge one another to be funnier and smarter.
It's high-energy play. It's the way friends
make love to one another.

Anne Gottlieb

T it for tat. Keeping score. Is that how you make sure things are fair? It's pretty draining isn't it? Sort of sucks the love out of everything! Yet so many couples use sex as a bargaining chip, money as a means of control—with no thought to the damage they do to love.

But what if you knew that you were both dedicated to giving to one another and to the relationship? And that your gifts, your help and your everyday work were received with loving appreciation? What if you both knew that you weren't being manipulated by "I'll do this only if you do that" as a way of life?

If the reward for your full, generous participation in your home life was the sincere satisfaction of loving well and being loved in the same way, would that be enough? If so, seek no other reward than love, and watch it flourish!

I will give and receive with no need for reward.

Our marriage was based on mutual
respect for each other's ideas, needs, wants and desires.
Our goal was to give and receive without
expectation of reward.

Richard Hoyt

READER/CUSTOMER CARE SURVEY

If you are enjoying this book, please help us serve you better and meet your changing needs by taking a few minutes to complete this survey. Please fold it and drop it in the mail.

As a special "**Thank You**" we'll send you news about new books and a valuable **Gift Certificate!**

PLEASE PRINT   C8C

NAME:_____

ADDRESS:_____

_____

TELEPHONE NUMBER:_____

FAX NUMBER:_____

E-MAIL:_____

WEBSITE:_____

(1) Gender: 1)_____Female 2)_____Male

(2) Age:
1)_____12 or under   5)_____30-39
2)_____13-15   6)_____40-49
3)_____16-19   7)_____50-59
4)_____20-29   8)_____60+

(3) Your Children's Age(s):
Check all that apply.
1)_____6 or Under   3)_____11-14
2)_____7-10   4)_____15-18

(7) Marital Status:
1)_____Married
2)_____Single
3)_____Divorced/Wid.

(8) Was this book
1)_____Purchased for yourself?
2)_____Received as a gift?

(9) How many books do you read a month?
1)_____1   3)_____3
2)_____2   4)_____4+

(10) How did you find out about this book?
Please check ONE.
1)_____Personal Recommendation
2)_____Store Display
3)_____TV/Radio Program
4)_____Bestseller List
5)_____Website
6)_____Advertisement/Article or Book Review
7)_____Catalog or mailing
8)_____Other_____

(11) What FIVE subject areas do you enjoy reading about most?
Rank: 1 (favorite) through 5 (least favorite)
A)_____ Self Development
B)_____ New Age/Alternative Healing
C)_____ Storytelling
D)_____ Spirituality/Inspiration
E)_____ Family and Relationships
F)_____ Health and Nutrition
G)_____ Recovery
H)_____ Business/Professional
I)_____ Entertainment
J)_____ Teen Issues
K)_____ Pets

(16) Where do you purchase most of your books?
Check the top TWO locations.
A)_____ General Bookstore
B)_____ Religious Bookstore
C)_____ Warehouse/Price Club
D)_____ Discount or Other Retail Store
E)_____ Website
F)_____ Book Club/Mail Order

(18) Did you enjoy the stories in this book?
1)_____Almost All
2)_____Few
3)_____Some

(19) What type of magazine do you SUBSCRIBE to?
Check up to FIVE subscription categories.
A)_____ General Inspiration
B)_____ Religious/Devotional
C)_____ Business/Professional
D)_____ World News/Current Events
E)_____ Entertainment
F)_____ Homemaking, Cooking, Crafts
G)_____ Women's Issues
H)_____ Other (please specify)_____

(24) Please indicate your income level
1)_____Student/Retired-fixed income
2)_____Under $25,000
3)_____$25,000-$50,000
4)_____$50,001-$75,000
5)_____$75,001-$100,000
6)_____Over $100,000

FOLD HERE

((25) Do you attend seminars?
1)_____Yes   2)_____No

(26) If you answered yes, what type?
Check all that apply.
1)_____Business/Financial
2)_____Motivational
3)_____Religious/Spiritual
4)_____Job-related
5)_____Family/Relationship issues

(31) Are you:
1) A Parent?_____
2) A Grandparent?_____

Additional comments you would like to make:

_____

_____

_____

_____

N-CS   C

Ever noticed that some days everybody and everything seems bleak, boring and worthless? And on other days it's just the other way around—everybody and everything appears happy and appealing, and life seems fresh and abundant? What makes the difference? Certainly, the outside world didn't flip upside down. It's you! You have the power to see with despair or with love.

However, when you're caught in a real funk, you can remember that you and the world are not always this way. You may not be able to change your vision for a time. You may be caught up in a mood, but even a mood has its place.

Practice seeing yourself, your spouse, everything and everyone else with the eye of love. When you cut into a strawberry, admire its inner beauty. When you change a tire, rejoice in the miracle of its invention. If you do, you will see the eye of love looking back at you.

I see through the eye of love.

The eye of love makes every person in the world friendly and attractive.

Sai Baba

In the early years of a relationship your challenges may seem overwhelming. Old habits, old allegiances may seem to cling with the weight of the world. You may want to give up. Love may seem out of your reach. But it's not.

You just have to remember that growth and change always occur in small increments. So, all you can do is confront an old belief that's holding you back, and work to turn it around.

Today, take one small step into love. If it's hard for you to call your lover to say "I love you," do it anyway. If you find it hard to apologize, but you were out of line last night, *make* the words "I'm sorry" come out of your mouth. If you're not sure you're worthy of love, take pride in the fact that you're reading this book to learn about your value. Then your future will be continually opening to love.

I grow my capacity for love with each step.

⁂

A journey of a thousand miles must begin with a single step.

Lao-tzu

Everyone thinks they know what's right for you. They're happy to pass on their words of wisdom, and angry when you don't follow them. Because they know what's right, right?

But the problem is—you're not them. And don't let anyone sell you short. Don't buy into limited thinking. Besides, what worked for them, or didn't work for them, doesn't apply to you. It's your desire and your commitment that will shape your life. Not statistics. Not a guru's divine wisdom. Not your parents' dreams for you. Only what you fiercely desire.

When you follow what you love, when you blaze your own trail, whether it's in your intimate relationship, your career, the way you raise a child, or even the friends you make— it's all the product of your vision, your pursuit, your inner guidance. Develop your inner strength and your unique character, and stay true to yourself and to your dream. And don't give up!

I trust and follow my deepest wisdom.

*At seventeen, I was told, "Better make all
the money you can in the next five years, because at
twenty-three you'll be all washed up."*

Joan Collins

We all have "unusualities"—sometimes so unusual we hide them. But when we marry, we no longer want to hide, so these behaviors start showing up—wanting to be loved.

It's so easy to mindlessly fall into contempt or fits of derisive laughter at our lover's "weirdness." But what for? Just to hurt the one we love? Just to act superior, as if our own stuff is all *Better Homes & Gardens* cover-page material? Remember, one of the reasons you chose to love your partner is because she stood out from the crowd, he had that special edge. But now, eating raw cookie batter, yelling at the television, meditating in the tub, pedicuring toenails while talking on the phone, and . . . you name it . . . are grounds for contempt rather than curiosity, honor and love.

You married one of a kind. The idiosyncrasies are part of the package. Change may not be out of the question. But why not open up and love the unusual, novel, singular, fun stuff?

I adore my lover's idiosyncrasies.

❧

Lately I've gotten into a horrible habit I'm ashamed of:
playing solitaire on the computer. It's a full-blown addiction,
but that's how I gather my thoughts—it's a Zen thing.

Teri Garr

How often do you comment on how great your spouse looks? How marvelous your wife's dinner tastes? How beautiful the car is after your partner waxed it? How fun it is to be with your husband? How often do you pay compliments to the one you love? Remember that compliments are just little ways of saying "I love you."

Start paying extra attention to all the things you like about your spouse. How she wakes you in the morning. The way he nuzzles the kids when he comes home. Her smell. His hug. The willingness to experiment with new foods. The capacity to really listen to you. Anything and everything that you admire, enjoy, like and are grateful for. Now put these observations into words. Not just once per item. Why be so stingy? Do it often.

Give several compliments every day. If your spouse shrugs off your compliments, insist that your expressions of love and respect be taken seriously. Be certain that your love is received!

I will be generous in complimenting my spouse.

I would dare say that the happiest relationships are probably the ones filled with the most compliments.

Michael Webb

Where is your focus? On the romantic and sexual behavior you want from your partner? Or on how you can be more loving? Do you imagine when you're both more successful, then you'll have the love you want? Or are you choosing to be as openhearted and loving as you can be today?

It's up to you. If you are constantly focused on what you don't have, or on what you'll have in the future, you're not available to love and be loved in this moment. You must choose to bring yourself into the heart of love, now. Do you balk at that idea? Are you insisting that your partner has to change first? If so, choose love now and see what happens.

Love is not a poker game, where you hide your hand and try to smoke out the other guy. Love is the game of life played for keeps. You are the only player you can control. Play the game of love with all your heart. Now.

**No matter what happens,
I choose to be loving today.**

*Romance and work are great diversions to
keep you from dealing with yourself.*

Cher

Basic to being human is the desire to be recognized and valued for who you really are. Yet, how often do you take each other for granted rather than open your curiosity to one another?

When it comes to conflict, get curious—not furious! When it comes to sex, become really intimate—get curious! No matter what the issue may be, you can never go wrong by getting more curious about your spouse. And don't forget to stay curious about yourself as well. After all, your lover can only recognize you through what you reveal, and sometimes she won't know the question to ask, or he'll assume he already knows the answer.

Make a list of questions you'd like to ask your spouse during a private dinner or while cuddled in bed. Then, when the time is right, turn on your full attention and ask away. Notice what a turn-on it is for both of you when you're deeply interested in your sweetheart.

**Curiosity is one of the best aphrodisiacs
I can give to love.**

Never lose a holy curiosity.

Albert Einstein

Y ou never choose your partner willy-nilly. In deciding to marry, you're responding to a spiritual wisdom that knows just the right kinds of experiences required for your learning and growth. When you marry it's inevitably to someone whose habits and behaviors provide just the right types of blessings and challenges for your journey of spiritual expansion.

Nothing in your marriage is an accident. It's all a perfect recipe for your self-development. If you're passive, you'll marry someone who's controlling. It will eventually force you to speak up and require your spouse to learn more respect. Your spouse might be super-organized and you're very hang-loose—you're perfect teachers for each other's need to get more balanced. There is always wisdom in your choice.

Write down several of the ways your spouse really bugs you. Now across from each item, describe how it's perfect for what you need to learn in response to it. Share your list with your spouse. Give thanks for the wisdom of your choice!

There is wisdom in my choice.

$\approx$

*There are no mistakes and it's never
boring on the edge of the imagination, which is only
pure spirit out having a bit of fun.*

Wavy Gravy

How often do you sincerely hug each other? Not just little, polite hugs, but the kind that stay with you long after you've gone your separate ways. The kind that cause you to give your whole body to the experience.

Hugging is highly underrated as an aphrodisiac—an aphrodisiac not just of your senses but of your spirit. When you both give yourselves to a passionate hug, your bodies absorb one another's energy, you connect skin to skin, you relax into one another. Your connection deepens and you join together in the surrender to love, need and support.

If you are not used to hugging with this intensity you may be embarrassed or feel awkward at first. Just remember, those feelings can also be deeply intimate and romantic when you express them honestly and with an open heart. Soon, you'll move past the awkwardness into deeper spiritual experiences of love that hugging has opened up for you.

I will give great hugs.

A warm hug from the one I love
absorbs all the pressures of my day.

Stuart A. Miller

83

Vulnerable. What a big word for open, accessible and exposed. Vulnerable. Without it, no one can see into your heart and soul. Without it, there can be no love.

Whoever gets taught that what's inside, deeply inside, is the lovable stuff? Didn't you grow up learning that it was your performance, your Little Mary Sunshine act or your Bobby Hipster routine that everybody "loved"? And it even passed pretty well in school—or so it seemed. But now, you're sick of all the anxiety and energy it takes to hold all that folderol together. And your spouse is, too.

Oh, good. Love will finally have a chance. Now you'll get to relax, let your hair down, as they say, and become vulnerable. Tell your truth. Feel the real feelings. Invite your spouse into the inside of the inside of your heart where love has been waiting. Today, and every day, practice being just who you are—without pretense—and see how your spouse reacts. Vulnerable—yes!

I am as vulnerable as I can be with my lover.

Using another as a means of satisfaction and security is not love.
Love is never security; love is a state in which there is no
desire to be secure; it is a state of vulnerability.

J. Krishnamurti

It's known as "my space." Unfortunately, taking one's space has a bad reputation because so many people assume that if their partner doesn't want to be with them every waking hour, then something must be wrong. In fact, something is wrong—there's no identity space in the universe that you inhabit.

As much as we are social beings needing closeness, we also need that psychic distance in which we are established as a Self. The difficulty arises when a partner interprets his spouse's desire for her own sense of being as a rejection of him, or her lover's need to stand individuated from her as his fear of commitment.

Solitude is not about time. It's not about being alone. Guarding your spouse's solitude means that you recognize, cherish and protect his or her otherness, that which is the basis of our being in the world.

I relish our alone times.

❧

A good marriage is that in which each appoints the other guardian of his solitude. A wonderful living side by side can grow up, if they succeed in loving the distance between them no less than one another.

Rainer Maria Rilke

One of the truly underrated romantic activities of our time is walking. Yes, walking. You can walk together for exercise. And that's great. But you can also go walking when you want to talk about something very sensitive and find it hard to be eye to eye. That way you can be shoulder to shoulder, comrades in love, facing a difficult challenge together the best way you know how.

Or, you can use walking as a romantic adventure. Pick a part of town you've never visited. Drive there. Make your way around the sights and scenes that interest you. Discuss the experiences you're having over a fun breakfast or lunch in a new café. As you open your awareness about various parts of your city, or the small towns around yours, be aware that you're also expanding your awareness of one another through these walking dates.

Sometimes you may want to just walk together in silence, listening for whatever wants to speak to you from within.

I treasure the intimacy when we're walking.

If you are seeking creative ideas, go out walking.
Angels whisper to a man when he goes for a walk.

Raymond Inmon

If you've ever felt like a failure at love, you know that love doesn't give up beckoning. It wants you. It wants you to change your mind about yourself and about love.

It doesn't matter how many times you've failed at love. It doesn't matter. Love offers you an open invitation to visit and get to know all that love might yield. All you need do is come to love again, opening to learn beyond the barren fields of your earlier days.

It isn't easy to come to love again and again. Yet, so many of us must because we never learned to open to love's calling. Instead, we learned to pull away. Just as love gave its heart to us, we pulled away in fear of being loved. Yet, once again alone, we felt the pull of love again, to come again to love. Yes, come again. Love is waiting for you. Just hold out your hand. Love is waiting for you. Come again.

I bring myself to love again and again.

Come, come, whoever you are,
Ours is not a caravan of despair.
Come even if you have broken your vow a hundred times
Come, come again, come.

Rumi

A ren't dogs remarkable!? Almost all dogs just light up, not only when their human family member approaches, but they light up just seeing you! They jump around, wagging their tails with joy and excitement. It's like they'd never met a human they didn't like.

Think what a different world it would be if each of us greeted one another in the same way. Oh, of course, we'd reserve our special greeting for those we dearly loved. But what if we delighted in one another's presence—at the market, in the office, just walking down the street. Wouldn't that be a treat!? Or have you been so wounded by people that the idea seems overwhelming? That's possible, too.

Just for today, experiment with greeting everyone you encounter with a smile, with a warm glance. Notice how you feel doing it, and how you are received. Decide how much of this "tail wagging" you want to continue doing in the future. And make sure to say hello to the dogs!

I can enjoy people the way dogs do.

❦

I see love with the wag of my dogs' tails.

Laurie LeClear

Cats are usually cautious about whom they like. Wild street cats, brought home to be domesticated, are even fussier about how soon they'll get friendly. Why? Because they're used to being on their own and now they're scared. Sound like anyone you know?

If you've ever loved a cat, you understand that a cat can only be the best cat it can be. You need to enter into its reality to have a meaningful relationship. You can't expect a cat to speak English, eat with a knife and fork, or even appreciate your humor. You can look into your cat's eyes and see what it's feeling. Then you can show your love so it fits the needs of your pet.

Now, why is it so tough to do the same thing with the person you love? Treat your mate's different ways like you do your cat's ways and love will become a purr-fectly delightful adventure.

**I can learn about respect for
differences from cats.**

*My cats, rescued from the streets, taught me about Being,
being my Self, a human, separate and unique from all others.
And about unconditional love, acceptance and forgiveness.*

Michael E. Hayne

You never thought it would come to this, did you? Your heartthrob is pointing out your flaws and coaching you how to do it better. What's going on here!? Life, love and the real world of relationships—unless you're too proud to learn from the one you love.

Who could know you better than your lover? Who could provide you with a bigger picture of who you could be than the person who sees you naked and scared? Deep, trusting love humbles you, over and over, in the most caring way, if you'll let it. When you give in to humility, you garner one of love's richest gifts—the gift of being loved into greatness. Don't let some false self-image, some defensive arrogance, block your availability to be a learner. Stay open. Keep learning.

Remember that learning in love is a two-way street. Learn from one another and vice versa—that's the only way it works.

I continually learn about myself from my lover.

*Humility is the acceptance of the possibility
that someone else can teach you something else you
do not know about yourself. Conversely, pride and
arrogance close the door of the mind.*

Arthur Deikman

"Be ye as little children, and come unto me." Sound stupid? Irresponsible? What could being like a kid have to do with living a good life and being spiritual?

What if the biblical verse means we need to give up being jaded, being soooooo sophisticated? What if these words invite us into the guileless open face of a child, the awe and amazement of a child watching a bird, the joyous shrieks of kids showering each other with the hose? What if being as little children is what allows us to be here and accept life as it is—and marvel in all that we get to experience and explore—instead of demanding that it be better, purer, our way?

Just for today, how can you view your world as a child? How can you abandon your need to be critical or above it all or socially polite—and replace it with unbridled spontaneity? What does your kid experience that you'd like to keep for every day?

I will help us see life as children do.

When I was a kid I drew like Michelangelo.
It took me years to learn to draw like a kid.

Pablo Picasso

So, you want to grow and heal your life. You want to learn more about love and spirituality. You want to have more meaning in your life. You want to know God, however you understand God to be. And you want to be loved for all that you are and love your partner in just the same way. Congratulations! Whether you're dating, in a new relationship or married—you've got the best love seminar in town!

No matter how much therapy you've had, how many books you've read, workshops you've attended—and they're all very helpful and can give you a model for how to proceed—you can't learn to love in a vacuum. You need to be in a relationship with someone where all your defenses get pushed, where you get scared, where someone loves you just for being you. That's where you can practice everything you've learned and more—much, much more.

Love the lessons of love—they provide you everything you want. And more—much, much more!

I appreciate the love seminar I'm in.

A partner will bring up all your patterns.
The truth is that your partner is your guru.
Don't avoid relationships: they are the best seminar in town.

Sondra Ray

How often do you listen to your spouse with 100 percent concentration? No concern with what you will say in return. No intention to correct or criticize. Only open curiosity and full awareness of your lover. When you do this, you surrender to the moment, you surrender to love.

When you can listen with total attention and careful interest, then conversation will follow like night follows day. You will be moved to speak, not because you need to make a point but because you will have been moved by what you've heard.

Beginning today, practice the art of mature listening. You can't do it when you're involved in another task. Mature listening requires your conscious heart and soul attention. It allows you to listen with your whole body. It's a gift to your spouse and to your love. Maybe you'll even call it listening with love!

I commit to listening to my spouse.

◈

*Listening is renouncing the impulse to direct
the other's attention to myself.*

Jacob Needleman

The issue of equality in romance comes down to commitment and creativity. There is no quick and easy recipe for an equality that fits all marriages. But evolving one is an equal-opportunity opportunity!

You and your partner have to negotiate—on an ongoing basis—your decision-making processes, a division of labor and the means for financial support. Your decisions must fairly and lovingly acknowledge and reflect the needs of the family as well as each of your skills, preferences and time availability.

For both of you to feel equal in your relationship, you both have to strive for maturity and love to guide your choices and behavior—not isolated independence or suffocating dependence. Real love is for grown-ups. Both of you must pitch in and do your share.

> **I define equality to suit the needs
> of our relationship.**

⚜

*Few Americans want to return to the days of
segregated gender roles and legal inequality, but they are
not sure how to build male-female intimacy ... in the midst of
the extremes of isolated self-sufficiency on the one
hand and codependency on the other.*

Stephanie Coontz

L ove can be really scary. Why? Because it asks us to give up wrong ideas about ourselves. But we don't want to change our identity. Clever defense mechanisms that pass for a self don't want to be exposed as frauds. But love insists we get real!

When you accept love into your heart, you must also surrender into the unknown. It may require that you give up trauma and drama, or loneliness or manipulation, with nothing but love to replace it. How boring, you may think! And, true, your life may become much calmer than ever before. That's because you are moving more and more into your center, into the truth of who you are.

Today, pay close attention to the areas of your identity that still go unloved, hidden behind pretense. What insecurities are you still so attached to? Can you give them up and open more fully to be loved? Can you say yes?

Being loved changes my identity.

❧

If I don't have my self-loathing, what do I have?

Janeane Garofalo

Whether you call it moral or sacred, spiritual or common sense, a truly successful relationship is ruled by one principle—"What would love do now?" Not "what's in it for me?" Not "how can I manipulate to get more than my share?" Not even "I'll go without to be a good person." Only what will be in both of our best interests. That's the best definition of love in action.

Love acts by doing. It never puts anyone down and never causes anyone intentional harm. Love is always an expression of greater good for everyone involved.

As you guide your day with the question, "What would love do now?" notice the times when your personality is in conflict with love's purposes. Ask yourself, "What is more important than love at this moment?" When you get the answer, ask again, "What would love do now?" and continue the process until love has won out and so have you.

I will guide my actions by what love would do.

✑

At the critical juncture in all human
relationships, there is only one question:
What would love do now?

Neale Donald Walsch

You may think you can trust someone right away. Maybe you think you can spot a schemer at first sight. Either way, on occasion, you may be correct. But the pleasure of living inside a trustworthy relationship must be developed and built over time. You have to teach one another and test each other and do so with patience and love.

Test one another?! Yes. The only way you learn you can trust someone is when you reveal things that are important, or ask for help and then see how your lover reacts. When you get less than you wanted, is there room for discussion and learning? Or are you ignored or laughed off? You must pay attention. You must be clear about what you need. You must be willing to negotiate so you're both satisfied. This is an ongoing process!

Reveal yourself, notice the response. Appreciate what is trustworthy. With patience and love, ask to change what is not.

I recognize that trust is built.

We have a very human need to believe, to trust each other.
I think we'd go mad if we felt there
was no one we could trust.

Leo Buscaglia

So many of us were taught that in order to win someone's love, we had to pretend to be something we weren't. "Put your best foot forward" meant "Don't show anything that would reveal your humanity." You believed it, and you've been suffering, because no one can see what's really lovable about you—including you.

If you are tired of suffering from lack of love, now's the time to abandon the game of "you hide" and "the other is supposed to seek." What will you lose? Just the hiding and seeking. But then you'll be accessible and lovable.

Easier said than done, you say. Too scary. What if you get rejected? Well, what if you do? The fact is you're already rejecting yourself by hiding who you are. It's time to invite your lover to love you for who you really are. So, starting today, show your spouse (bit by bit) how you truly feel, what really pleases you, how lonely you've been. What do you have to lose?

I will face losing to gain love.

❧

When the fear of losing myself became
greater than the fear of losing the man I love,
I risked exposing myself and my fear.
The result: I finally became accepted and
loved for who I truly am.

Pat Feinman

Lots of people get into a relationship with the attitude, "What's in it for me?" Many others lose themselves by caretaking everyone but themselves. Some people swap these roles back and forth. Either way, you may say you're in a relationship, but you're really alone.

To be intimate, to experience real romance, you have to be able to give and receive simultaneously. You must experience your own desire and pleasure while, at the same time, contributing to those of your spouse. Otherwise, it's either self-centered greed or selfless sacrifice.

Plan a romantic event for tonight that you know will pleasure you both—giving each other massages, making love, feeding each other ice cream. At some point, take turns describing the dual realities of 1) how your spouse has pleasured you and 2) how providing pleasure to your spouse has been just as important.

I know that both of us matter.

⬥

If I am not for myself, who will be for me? If
I am only for myself, what am I?

Rabbi Hillel

*The biggest mistake is
believing there is one right way
to listen, to talk, to have conversation
—or a relationship.*

DEBORAH TANNEN

How long has it been since you did a thorough clean-out of your closets, storage areas and garage? Are they stuffed with old outfits you never wear, shoes that never fit, gifts you never liked, memorabilia that you no longer care about?

Make a date to do a massive clean-out of your home. You won't be just getting rid of a lot of junk, you will be opening the space for new abundance to join you. Whether you work together, consulting back and forth, or you work in different areas at the same time—know that your clean-out is a love gift to your relationship.

Make sure you provide goodies that will help the clean-out be more fun. Play your favorite music. Get together a special lunch, great snacks and drinks ahead of time. And when you're done, pack up your former treasures, take them to your local thrift shop and get a tax deduction receipt. Then rent a romantic video and celebrate arm in arm on the couch.

I will make a love date to clean out the closets.

❧

Cluttered closets mean a cluttered mind.
As you clean the closet, say to yourself, "I am cleaning
the closets of my mind." The Universe
loves symbolic gestures.

Louise Hay

All that you share, all that you know about each other, that is what you're sewing into your love. These are the stitches that hold together the fabric of your particular love. That's why no two loves can ever be the same, for they are never created quite the same way.

Every effort you make to work out your differences, every fun-filled break in your routine adds to the love you share. Each of these are gold and silver threads you are consciously stitching into your love. All of these actions can make your relationship more valuable to each of you, as long as you understand that love is always co-created, never dropped on you fully formed.

Nothing you do in your relationship is without consequence. You are always adding a new stitch, making the seams stronger, or you are pulling out threads, tearing apart what you have. It's an expression of your value and it's your choice.

I invest in my love every day.

It is threads, hundreds of tiny threads, which sew people together through the years. That is what makes a marriage last —more than passion or even sex.

Simone Signoret

Responsibility and love. What do they have to do with each other? Maybe you're thinking, "Okay, here comes the lecture." Sounds just like your parents, right? So, being responsible may sound stodgy, dull, old-fashioned. And you just want to have fun!

Real love is fun. But don't confuse partying, bowling, travel and long days at the beach with the fun of love. The fun that love offers is only available when you are in charge of yourself, when you are response-able: able-to-respond to any of the gazillion situations that can arise in a committed relationship; able-to-respond from an awareness of what is good and right for you; able-to-respond with compassion and care for yourself and the one you love.

Today, practice self-responsibility all day. Make sure you are aware of what you need, what will fulfill you and what will feel like emotional, intimate fun. Then do whatever you can to realize your fulfillment.

I accept full responsibility for my life.

I am the author of my situation and
I am responsible for the fulfillment of my desires.
Nobody was born to serve my needs.

Nathaniel Branden

Gardening can be a joyous expression of nurturing new life or it can be a royal drag. It's all in how you do it. If it's just a chore, forget about it. But as an act of love—what a blessing to the spirit of your marriage.

Nurture the health and soul of your love by sharing in the planting and caretaking of some of nature's beauty. If you have a yard or patio, springtime is great for planting gorgeous blooms. If you're limited to houseplants, pick them out together. View your plants as an extension of your family, rather than just the shrubs that make your home more attractive.

As you work together, pay attention to the way each of you expresses your love to the wonders of nature, the care, the tender handling of life. Each of you is blooming in the process and your own roots are growing ever more entwined. Enjoy your own blossoming!

I enjoy our plants and flowers together.

*We love to plant spring flowers and marvel
at each other's inner and outer beauty, while we
admire the beauty of God's bouquet.*

Art Klein and Pat Feinman

It used to be that you knew who you were because of the place in which you were born, or the land you called home. But more and more, people are transient, moving every few years, never really having a home. Business and chat can now even be conducted in no place—the Internet. Many people feel anonymous. Invisible.

For your spouse's identity to feel secure, she needs to know that she belongs in your life. He needs to know that he has a home within your heart. Wounds of the heart are often committed because of a devastating injury to one's identity. When your spouse ignores you, dismisses you, makes you irrelevant—your whole being has been wiped out. Enraging! So, be very conscious about your lover's identity.

To support your spouse's sense of identity, describe specific examples about how your life could never be as fulfilling without the blessings of her presence in your life, his involvement in your world. Identity is precious. Handle with care.

I commit to supporting my lover's identity.

The issues of anonymity and identity are the
central spiritual and psychological challenge of our time.

Jack Whalen

Relationships can really be frustrating, and sometimes downright difficult. Sadly, most people give up right away, as if marriage were a ride at an amusement park, designed and run by other people. The attitude seems to be: don't like the ride, get off, go to the next ride. But you are the co-designer and half of the construction and management team. If you just go to the next ride, it will still be your co-creation. So, why not create a new design?

While re-creating your relationship, don't give up. And, remember—persist, persist, persist. If you give up, you never learn to do it differently. But if you keep learning from each other and from your mistakes, you'll get better at communicating, fighting fair and receiving love. You'll get better at being yourself. And you'll become more and more lovable.

If there's love between you, don't give up!

I commit to trying one more time.

❧

Our greatest weakness lies in giving up.
The most certain way to succeed is to always
try just one more time.

Thomas A. Edison

Greeting cards can be so saccharin, so sickeningly sweet. Others are nasty and hostile in the name of humor. Some are boring and simpleminded. It can be very difficult to find a card that's just right for the one you love.

Yet, there are many special holidays, birthdays and anniversaries that invite the intimacy of a great card. Don't overlook the romance in finding the card that will touch his soul, or light up her eyes. Take time to search for the card that speaks directly to your spouse's personality and interests. Stretch yourself. Don't just grab a card "that will do." Make your search a love gift. And if you still can't find the right one, then get a blank card and make up your own loving message. Even if you're not a great writer, your courage and love will shine right through.

Give the gift of caring, and care enough to find the very best card you can. The little things do count!

**I will give my spouse more emotionally
intimate cards.**

*My husband picks out cards that touch my heart and we usually
end up in tears. This is a special way we're intimate with each
other. (Most of my cards bring us to tears, too.)*

Laura Whitledge

I t's so easy to forget that you not only love each other, but that you are a blessing to each other's lives. Then the days go by, followed by the passing years, and then one day there's only one of you, alone, grieving.

What will you miss, then, that you take for granted today? What funny quirk or irritating habit will you remember—and wish you'd laughed more and complained less? For death is right around the corner, whether it's tomorrow or fifty years from now. And it invites you to give your heart more fully in every living moment you have left together.

Don't start dying before it's time. Don't grieve for what never happened; that just makes you old before your time. Start this day living with love for the time you have together. If it needs some lovework to make it better, don't put it off. Do it now, so that your days together are blessings, every day.

I value every moment we have with each other.

⊱

We are together nearly twenty-four hours a day.
We work, play, eat and sleep together. At our age we are
realizing how short life really is and we savor every
moment in each other's presence.

Ron and Susan Scolastico

The emotions of love are infinite. Yet sometimes when you look inside to speak, there is nothing. So you are silent. But your heart aches to connect, to say something. You search again. Perhaps you notice something. But a jumble of confusion provides no help.

No one in love is ever silent or evasive just to torment his beloved or manipulate her heart's desire. Mostly, people in love who seem to have difficulty communicating are doing just that—having difficulty communicating. Why? Because they don't know what to say. Why? Because they don't know what they feel. They may be overwhelmed by a torrent of topsy-turvy emotions. Or they may be terrified of feeling much of anything. Love does that to humans.

Be patient with one another. Do not push love to speak, for the heart can only reveal its truth when it is ready. Are you ready to hear the voice of love when it speaks to you?

I can always speak what's in my heart.

When you are in love and you don't know what to say, say what's in your heart.

Tom Justin

To make it more fun to learn about the different ways you and your spouse see the world, try playing "Up Telescope." When you see a movie or go to a party or whatever, don't just go home and hide your perceptual "telescopes" under your bed. Spend some time listening to each other describe the theme and characters in the movie, the relationships between the party guests, the main point of the lecture. Give your full attention to looking through each other's telescopes to see how different your experiences were.

To do this with love, there can be no debate or argument about what you experienced. The point is to get as close a look as you can to how each of you sees the world differently from one another.

"Up Telescopes" is handy to break down a conflict you're having as well. The goal is to get inside each other's experiences without giving up who you are. Two points of view for the price of one!

I open myself through my spouse's point of view.

※

The best we can do is not prevent ourselves
from trying each other's telescopes.

Warren Farrell

Your life is no doubt crammed with work, errands, kids' needs, housekeeping and all kinds of things that make it difficult to focus on romance. But you could take five minutes each day to devote to love. Right? Right!

Give five minutes every day to think about the person you love. Reflect on what his needs are, what her current intimacy concerns might be. Are you available for your beloved in a loving way? It's so easy to go through your day without giving any real thought to your spouse. It may even be difficult to think about your mate without relating it back to your own needs. But don't cheat the one you love.

Find and set a time to tune in to your partner. Perhaps you'll do it together, about one another, snuggled in each other's arms first thing in the morning. Just open your heart, and receive whatever comes to you. Let it guide you to greater intimacy and care!

**I will take five minutes a day to
meditate on my relationship.**

*Just five minutes a day in private
meditation on your lover can do wonders to keep
your heart open and your love alive.*

Kim Fong

There's so much talk about commitment in marriage, and the fear of it. So let's be clear. Healthy commitment to love and marriage is not a commitment to your spouse; if so, you'd have to give up your life if your spouse suddenly left or passed away. And commitment is not a lock that forces you to stay together no matter what. That's just emotional imprisonment. These are the concepts of commitment that scare people to death.

But what about committing to the lifelong creation of your love? When you commit to cultivating your relationship—so that it benefits both of you emotionally and expands you both spiritually—why wouldn't you want to do that for the rest of your life? That commitment respects where you are today and invites you into the future—in love—together.

Make a date to honor your love with new commitment vows. Then celebrate! You might want to take these vows every year on your anniversary, or even every month!

I commit totally to my marriage.

Commitment means, "I am going to stick with you
and support your experience of well-being."

Stewart Emery

If you're "attached" to your spouse, it suggests you are stuck. Just like nailing a curtain rod to the wall. The problem is that without the wall the rod falls down.

Are you attached to your spouse in a way that feels like, "I can't live without her," or "Without him, I'm nobody"? If so, you're codependently hooked. You're fused to one another rather than committed to your marriage. In a committed love, each of you is capable of taking care of yourselves. You have value with or without a marriage. But with attachment, your lack of value and worldly competence is reconfirmed to you every day. Eventually the wall gets tired of supporting the rod and the rod will get sick of decorating the wall. Then, welcome to divorce court.

Develop your ability to function independently from your spouse. At the same time, focus on the love you feel rather than the need. Leave attachment behind and grow into mature love.

**I want to live my life with you,
not make you my life.**

Attachment means, "I am stuck without you."

Stewart Emery

A s you think and speak, so shall you live. Become acutely aware of your negative thoughts and verbal messages that prohibit a positive response or outcome in your relationship. Beware how you condemn your spouse into forever disappointing you, with phrases like, "You never, ever do . . . ," or "I can never trust you to . . ." Your words design the blueprint and instruction manual for your spouse's failure.

The next time you get into a conflict, take a few moments and change your thinking from "This is hopeless!" to "We can do this differently, it will just take some time for us to figure it out." Speak the two different messages to yourself right now. Can you feel how the first cuts off any new possibility? And the second opens you to learning?

Stay aware of the messages you deliver to your lover. As you speak, you reap the rewards of your messages—for good or not. Be loving. Be wise!

My words determine my reality.

"What you say is what you get in the Oceans of Emotions,"
said the Crab to Destiny the Little Dragon.

Nicole K. Clark and John T. Clark
(From *The Oceans of Emotions*)

Whe you're in love, when you're starting your family, death seems very far away. But it's not. At least in terms of being responsible for the possibility, especially if you have children.

You may think it's not very romantic to talk about death. Yet it can be intensely intimate if you share your fears, your concerns and face into what death means to both of you. So, from time to time, sit down together and discuss what you want to have happen if either or both of you die or become disabled. Make sure you have a will that is up to date. Plan for the guardianship of your children. Don't leave anything to fate. Document and tape record your directives. Taking care of your family, in advance of any tragedy, can be a very loving and intimate experience.

Make sure you stay emotionally open and connected during your discussions. Notice how much you would miss your spouse if death shattered your marriage.

I commit to creating a will, estate
and guardianship plan.

Every so often, you need to have a "financial fire drill."

Janet Bodnar

Perhaps you already have a savings account, a retirement account and other investments. Maybe not. But what if you started a Fun Money Savings Account—or whatever the two of you would call it? You could earmark this money for romantic weekends, vacations, the beginnings of a savings account or whatever turns you on.

Get a big, playful container. Decide all the ways it'll be fun to throw money in. For instance, at the end of each day, you both throw in your change. Any money you find on the street. The difference between the sale price of your purchase and the regular price. A dollar a day each. Savings from coupons at the market. The savings from uncancelled stamps on your mail, cut off and reused. Whatever would be fun and not curb your lifestyle, so you're both joined in the romance of saving money—together.

Money, honey, I've got you! Yes, you can have it all— money, your honey—and however you want to play with it!

We can save fun money.

❧

*We squirrel away our daily change and
toss in the savings when we get a great buy.
That's our play money.*

Modina and Jamal Jefferson

We live in a very contemptuous society. In the media, in the news, on the world stage, there's the constant voice of arrogance, righteousness and disrespect for individuality.

How often do you catch yourself rolling your eyes at your lover's behavior, just because it's not your way? How often do you slam your partner, just because he goofed up in some unimportant way, just because she didn't do it as well as you would have? Look inside yourself—what's the need for contempt? Does it make you feel any better about yourself? Doubtful. Does it inspire your beloved to greater things, to going that extra mile the next time? Hardly. It's long overdue for you to give up being contemptuous—of anyone.

As soon as you catch yourself feeling contemptuous (and you may need your partner to help by pointing it out a few times), put on the brakes, and find a more compassionate, helpful response. Make love, not war!

I replace contempt with curiosity.

Teach not thy lips such scorn;
for they were made for kissing,
not for such contempt.

Shakespeare, *Richard III*

How often do you hold hands, hug or otherwise touch each other affectionately in public? Do you let your friends and family see you looking at each other with love and admiration? Or do you hide your enjoyment of one another? If so, ask yourself, what do you cherish as more important than enjoying one another in public? Whose opinion of you counts more than your love?

When you're affectionate in public, you stay connected in a very warm and caring way. If you walk down the street holding hands, you're saying to each other and everyone who sees you, "I'm glad I'm with you!" If you lovingly gaze at each other during a dinner party, you make it clear that your love is solid. And it's fun! You stay young at heart. Just be sure your public affection is just that: affection, not sexual foreplay.

Enjoy each other in public. Be an example for others. Let your love shine!

I commit to being affectionate in public.

Children, friends and neighbors need to see more couples
holding hands and gazing into each other's eyes.
Don't be ashamed of your love, flaunt it!

Michael Webb

Of course you've heard the story of Adam and Eve, the Apple and the Snake. And no doubt you heard that it was Eve who ruined Adam's life by getting him to take a bite out of that blankety-blank apple.

But what if that's a story for earlier times? What if life in the Garden was too perfect and God saw that Adam and Eve weren't taking personal responsibility for their spiritual growth? So he sent out the Snake, a stand-in for Wisdom, to introduce the next Epoch of Soul Growth. Remember the Apple was the fruit of the Tree of Good and Evil—Adam and Eve now had the power of choice! They had to make it in the world, as a team, on their own. God now required that Adam and Eve grow up and leave behind their childish ways, depending upon the Father to take care of everything.

God gave Adam and Eve, all of us, relationship to help us grow up. Use God's gift wisely. Love well.

My relationship is a gift from God.

Relationship is the greatest gift God
ever gave to you.

Neale Donald Walsch

More and more couples are working together, whether it's out of their home or in the corporate world. For some people, this will never be attractive. But for many of us, working with our spouse is heaven.

The trick to working together, even if it's just around the house, is to respect that each of you has differing skills and talents, preferences and dislikes. When you get the hang of trusting and respecting that each of you is contributing roughly fifty-fifty, you can relax, do the tasks you're best at and divide up those that neither of you likes (or hire someone for those). Treat each other with the same respect you would a colleague and remember you share the same goals of personal and financial success.

That you are different from each other is a blessing. Your differing input can keep you balanced. Learn from each other's excellence. Negotiate the challenges for the benefit of the company and your marriage. Welcome cooperation into your life together!

We complement each other's talents.

*There's nothing better than working with
someone you know loves you.*

Robin Wright Penn

The capacity of our marriages to expand our lives is so vast, we cannot even imagine it. Yet, we usually stick our relationships into tidy boxes of daily habits and weekend "have-to's" that are killing the incredible potential of our coupling.

Don't play it so safe. Make your marriage into a long-term discovery cruise. Because you are very different from each other, you can never get bored unless one or both of you isn't showing up to be discovered. Between the inside (personal) and the outside (public) discovery possibilities, love can be the most exciting event in your life. Not just cozy and safe. Not just socially comfy. But the best spiritual adventure of your life.

Today, start planning some new outside expeditions: in your city, your state and worldwide if you have the time and money. Also, plan a personal expedition to tell each other stories about your childhoods that you've never told before. Open yourself to discovery.

My marriage is a continual discovery.

We discovered in each other and ourselves
worlds, galaxies, a universe.

Anne Rivers Siddons

The demands of perfectionism rob you of love. You can never relax and just do your best, whatever that may be. You have to know everything—now. You have to be better than everyone else—now. Being who you are and doing your best just doesn't cut it. So there's no way for love to get in. Because you can't believe you deserve it.

But all you can ever be is who you are—and that has to be good enough, because you cannot be anything else! When you understand this, you begin to accept yourself as is. Please understand that being your best takes extra effort, whether it's staying aware of current events, working out, having hobbies, taking care of your family, excelling in your career. Whatever makes your life meaningful, do it well.

Today, give your best to every activity. When you stretch yourself, and know that you aren't holding back, you increase your ability to love yourself and become available to receive your partner's love.

I give my best to all activities.

❧

Doing the best at this moment puts you in
the best place for the next moment.

Oprah Winfrey

Everyone knows that regular exercise is good for your physical health. But it's also a great boost to your overall vitality, longevity and sex life. Can't beat that, right? Do the two of you "take it to the mat" together several times a week—however you may do it? If so, great! Keep it up!

The beauty of working out together is that you get to enjoy each other's company while feeling supported to stay in shape (or pound the extra weight off, if that's your goal). If you're beginners, start slowly. Take a short walk after dinner. Work your way up to a routine that fits your daily interests. Take dancing lessons. Play tennis together. Swim at the local Y. You can work out at home with a video guide or a book on yoga.

Be creative. Have fun. Value your love enough to get both of you out there moving around, working up a sweat, getting your hearts pounding—for health and for each other!

I commit to doing regular exercise together.

❧

*Marriage gives you a built-in
workout buddy.*

Abby King

Hearts and flowers, trips to Tahiti, hours of passionate lovemaking—that's romance, right? But what about washing the dishes together, the little private jokes you share, respecting each other's personal alone time? Or do you take those for granted, missing the aliveness of your love as it is expressed from moment to moment?

Do not cheat romance. It's available far more often than you may think. It's in every small and large way you consciously appreciate each other, share the tasks, have fun together. Does that sound too mundane? Too ordinary? Well, at first it might seem that way. After all, we've all grown up on a steady diet of movies and books that portray romance as swept-away passion coupled with extravagant gifts and trips. But that's just fantasy romance. True romance is available every time you consciously connect with your partner and treasure the moment.

Hold your heart open to each kindness, each touch that you exchange with your spouse and feel the romance—the true romance today!

I celebrate our intimacy with gusto.

Is not this the true romantic feeling—not to desire to escape life, but to prevent life from escaping you?

Thomas Wolfe

While your lover's words and actions can be hurtful and even mean-spirited, they cannot make you feel bad about yourself—unless some part of you believes you deserve shabby treatment. No matter the insult that's thrown at you, if there's no place for it to land inside you, it can't take up residence. When you really understand this, you stop giving away your power to other people.

One of the blessings of a good marriage is that it can function like an emotional workout lab. Because you can be emotionally vulnerable with your spouse, old inferiority feelings are likely to surface from time to time. With the loving help of your spouse, these feelings can be recognized as coming from your past experiences and then healed by your spouse's respect and care. For the healing to occur, you must exercise receiving your spouse's loving opinion of you, rather than clinging to your feelings of inferiority.

Know that you determine your value. Today, notice all of the ways you are worthwhile.

No one else can make me feel bad about myself.

No one can make you feel inferior
without your consent.

Eleanor Roosevelt

You are never powerless in your relationship. There is always something you can do to change things. Even if that means leaving your relationship. But far too many people stay in relationships, despairing of ever being happy, of ever feeling loved. Don't do it. Your life is too precious to lose it to despair.

What can you do differently? What action can you take? How can you change the way you live so you are more assertive, so that your spouse takes notice and changes as well? How can you make yourself more approachable, more available to your partner? How can you earn respect in your own eyes for showing up as a full partner, rather than vanishing in despair on the sidelines?

Take some action today that will change how you feel about yourself. Push yourself to do something that changes your habit(s) in some way. Walk through the fear and anxiety, they're only feelings. Life awaits on the other side. Take action!

Today I will take constructive action.

❧

Action is the antidote to despair.

Joan Baez

Problems in your love life occur in the differences between you and your partner, between your fantasies and reality. In the ways you're alike or similar, it's cozy, comfy, warm and snugly, right?

So we enter marriage unconsciously fearful of one another's different ways. In the beginning we gloss over them, thinking they're cute, adorable or charming. Then months or years later our fear has the best of us. "Irreconcilable differences" land us in divorce court.

But that doesn't have to happen. All you have to do is change your vision of differences to lose the fear. Reality need not be "us" versus "them." You can see the world in a spiritually expansive way, so that both of your realities have value. Then, differences exist to help you have a more exciting, fascinating and growth-filled marriage. (Think how boring it would be if you and your spouse were exactly alike.)

I am releasing my fear of differences.

❧

We're frightened of what makes us different.

Anne Rice

Who are your friends? Do you, as a couple, have loving, supportive couples and individuals with whom you socialize? Or are your friends more of a pity party, people you go to for solace and reinforcement that there's nothing you can do about your marriage except feel sorry for yourself?

The quality of your friends is important. When you associate with couples and singles who value the lovework necessary for deep intimacy and practice it in their lives, your relationship is surrounded by a current of loving strength. When your so-called friends can't support your marriage and the work it takes to keep both of you growing together, you cheat yourself of the love you could have—both in the quality of your friendships and in your marriage.

Take stock of your friendships. Are they healthy, life-enhancing relationships that support your marriage? Or are there some people, perhaps from a former time, who need to be cut loose so your love and your life can better grow?

Today I look at my choice of friends.

❧

The first step to self-enhancement and opening new doors is choosing wise relationships.

James Melton

I n the movies it seems like once you meet the "right one," everything is set in place and it will last that way forever. Of course, life and love are never like that. In fact, when we allow ourselves to open to love's powers, and the supportive encouragement of our spouse, the more we become willing to move beyond our fears to expose the wonderfully appealing and engaging truth of who we are.

In fact, the marriages that are most fulfilling are those in which both people join together to develop themselves, to become all that they can be, so that their life together is an always-unfolding adventure. Each of them is continually growing as they grow together.

In what ways do you hold back from fully revealing yourself? How do you hold back from creating a deeper intimacy in your life? Today, consider how you might let down your guard. The love you receive will also be your own.

I am always becoming.

⁍

To be what we are, and to become what we are capable of being—that is the only creed worthy of life.

Robert Louis Stevenson

Was your parents' marriage set on automatic pilot? Was every day pretty much alike? Dependable and predictable and very boring. Perhaps you vowed never to live like that.

In today's world, there is more freedom than ever before to create your relationship the way you want. How do you do that? By learning. That's what love demands. You need to learn about yourself, your spouse, your finances, your changing tastes and interests, your children and more. To keep love alive you need to be continually learning. It's such a blessing, because it's the very same thing you need to live a full and meaningful life.

Today, learn something new about how you love your lover. Make a list of all the wonderful attributes you love or make a list of all the ways your lover blesses your life. Then, tonight, share your list. Make sure you both are conscious that you are learning more about each other as you make love out of bed.

I continually learn about my lover.

❧

When one is in love one is learning, the
two conditions cannot be separated.

Robert Sardello

May

When ye unite with another,
do so with deep consciousness of the
dignity of that which you do.
Give yourself to this work of love,
with your souls and with your minds,
even as with your flesh.

OMAR HALEBY

When we first fall in love, during those bliss-filled days, we can feel as one. There are no conflicts or hurt feelings. Then the differences begin showing up along with the challenges they provide. Oneness fades. Yet, you still yearn to feel that undefinable connection that melts the boundaries, that propels you into realms of spiritual wholeness.

You can get there. You really, really can. Not by trying to get back to the way you felt at the beginning, but by discovering each other over and over, ever more deeply. Use what you learn to love more fully, to know each other in the private places that no one else will ever know. It's there, in those delicate and tender knowings that the eternal spirit of love brings you into a oneness that can never be destroyed.

Attempts to find oneness by obliterating your partner's individuality, his or her solitude, and vice versa results in codependency and ultimately resentment. Oneness is only accessible through the twoness.

Through our twoness I find our oneness.

This oneness, gradually accomplished
throughout a lifetime in twoness, is the highest
achievement of time or eternity.

D. H. Lawrence

They say that "love is wasted on the young." That's not true. The young love as best they can, because, after all, they are young.

Love, however, insists we outgrow our youth, move through the fantasies of romantic bliss, discover the magic waiting in the differences between us and emerge into the spiritual wonder of mature love. Through love we are stretched beyond old comfort zones, expanded to hold more love than we ever thought possible to receive. Through love we are remade over and over again. Through love we celebrate ourselves as we celebrate life.

If you don't want to be remade through love, then settle for less. But if love calls to you and you answer, you must release your attachment to who you've known yourself to be and be remade again and again.

I am being remade by love.

When people are truly in love, they experience far more
than just a mutual need for each other's company and consolation.
In their relation with one another they become different people....
They are made over into new beings.

Thomas Merton

However close and loving you may be today, there's always more romance and intimacy for the two of you to discover. Love keeps changing you and you keep changing your love all life long.

Do you have a dream of how it will be in a few years, or when you're in your later years? Don't just go along without a vision of what you want. Dream. Dream of the deeper tenderness you want to experience. Dream of how your sexuality can become more vulnerable, your humor and play more fun. Dream of dancing in the moonlight, of holding each other in the final years—remembering all that you shared, all that you learned together. Dream!

Dream your dreams together. Share them. Talk about them. Add to them as you grow. Let your dreams teach you and color the way you love each other. Commit to the fulfillment of your dreams—together!

I commit to creating and holding our dream.

❦

*No dream was ever accomplished
without the dream.*

Julia McIver

It doesn't matter how you pray or meditate, or whether you even believe in prayer. What matters is that you agree on some time together when you give over your attention and your energy to the Larger Forces or God, however you understand the energies that run the lawfulness of the planet.

Whether in prayer or meditation, you may want to add to your experience by visualizing that you already have what you desire. Perhaps you want better careers—more self-expression, recognition and monetary reward—or you want to be less angry. During this time of contemplation, show yourself and your God what you want by imagining that you have it. Feel this in your body. Know it is true.

While you give gratitude for what you have, you also communicate what you want. Do this together on a regular basis, with special candles, incense, music, whatever is meaningful to you both, and you will experience the loving power of spiritual regeneration.

**When we pray or meditate together,
we are divinely connected.**

❧

*Before every meal they bowed their
heads and gave thanks, marveling at their blessings:
a wonderful family, good fortune and each other.*

Laura Allen

138

Were you taught that it isn't nice to be selfish? To never hurt anyone's feelings? To go without if others are in need? Too often these injunctions to be without a self have passed for the definition of love. But if you're always going without, if you can never feed your own soul, if everyone else comes first, where do you find the abundance to give and to love?

Me, me, me!!! Yes, you have to count. You have to be a solid half of the equation in your marriage. You must also be attentive and respectful to the other half—the love of your life. Of course! But do not ever leave yourself out. Your marriage needs you. So does the person who chose to marry you. You. Not someone else, not a pale stand-in for your character and personality. You.

Today, make sure that you—your feelings and your well-being—are always considered in what you choose to do.

Today I pay attention to me.

⁂

I cannot give you the formula for success,
but I can give you the formula for failure—
which is: Try to please everybody.

Herbert Bayard Swope

You may think that conflict is dangerous. Someone has to win and someone has to lose. You may be all too familiar with shouting matches or the silent and deadly treatment. But those are the knee-jerk strategies of the uninformed and the unconscious.

Conflict is simply the clash of differences, inevitable between any two people in an intimate relationship. As long as you both care for each other, there's no need for panic and no reason to pull out your artillery. The point is for each of you to understand as clearly as possible what each of you feels, needs and wants. You'll each have to grow and change in some way(s) to better serve the emotional needs of your relationship, but that's the beauty of conflict. When approached with respect for each other as uniquely different individuals, conflict ultimately opens you to deeper awareness of each other's vulnerabilities. Then a stronger and more loving intimacy can be established each and every time you work out a conflict.

Today, remember that conflict is an unavoidable part of intimacy and growth. Open your mind and heart to conflict as a spur to the depth and breadth of your relationship.

I can approach conflict with openness and courage.

Conflict is ignorance searching for consciousness.

Brian Muldoon

Conflicts can be very healthy when they are resolved in a way that benefits both of you, helping your relationship grow and expand. To do this, you must be willing to respect that there is another side to the fight besides your own. You already know what you're upset about. But do you really, really know what your spouse is so mad about?

Lots of people pay lip service to listening to their spouse. But real love demands that you understand and value your lover's feelings, beliefs and behaviors as importantly as you value your own. And vice versa. Now you have the basis on which to become creative and invent a new way to be together around the issue at hand.

Use conflict constructively. Care about your spouse's feelings and concerns. Then open yourself to a new way to be together, a way that expands your love and your life.

Both our points of view have to count.

$\approx$

Real communication occurs when we can see ...
from the other person's point of view, to sense how it feels to him,
to achieve his frame of references in regard to
the thing he is thinking about.

Carl Rogers

How often do you goof around together, all silly and falling down with laughter? Or have you turned adulthood into a static ode to dullsville?

One of the great freedoms that a committed, lasting love can offer is the room to play, to invent private jokes, to dance in the aisle at the grocery market or to sing off-key at the tops of your lungs. You may think you're too busy to indulge in these frivolous activities. But they don't take time, they just require your desire to play with each other and have fun—however the two of you do it. Maybe you've forgotten how, or you never were silly. Thankfully, it's never too late to reinvent having a good time.

Today, do zany things, stuff you've never thought about before. Make bets on who can look the sweatiest after gardening. Take photographs for evidence. Eat dessert before dinner. . . . Enjoy!

I enjoy the fun we have together.

∞

*It is only when you see people looking ridiculous that
you realize just how much you love them.*

Agatha Christie

A vacation of love creates a sacred geography—both in your heart and in the place of your visit. It doesn't require a lot of money to have a great getaway, only love for each other and love of travel. When you make exploration of love one of your goals, along with meandering through the roads and byways of your destination, then every aspect of your trip can be a way to explore the larger forces of life.

Notice the heart and poetry of your sacred geography. The ocean waves move into the shore and away, always returning to kiss the beach once more. A panoramic view invites you to journey further into the mystery of life. A beggar reminds you of your gratitude, a cathedral of The One joining you together, a great meal invites you to taste more of life's abundance.

Begin to plan your next vacation—with the sacred geography of your love at the top of the itinerary.

I will plan vacations of love.

*We ate well and cheaply and drank well
and cheaply and slept well and warm together
and loved each other.*

Ernest Hemingway

When you allow love to open your heart and sweep you into the midst of life's blessings, you behold one of the central miracles of this life—the miracle of love's power to transform you. You begin to see the wonder in everything.

Everyday events become miracles of beauty and creation. You were alone. Then you found someone who loves you for who you really, really are. And you feel the same way about your lover. A miracle takes your breath away. Sometimes your life together will be painful, yet miraculously the pain will open you to see life as a richer blessing than before. The joy you share will bless all you know.

Your existence is a marvelous manifestation of God's grace—otherwise known as a miracle. Open yourself to the miracles that surround you every day. Expect them and they will come. Bless them with gratitude and they will dance for your applause with even more joy.

I experience the miracle of love every day.

❧

Anyone who doesn't believe in
miracles is not a realist.

David Ben-Gurion

Once you bring a child into your marriage, sometimes you must divide your attention. Often parents believe the needs of their children should come first, with their marriage coming in a slow second. Don't do this. If you do, you will sacrifice the intimacy and romance needed to continually grow your marriage, and you give your children the power to run the family.

Your children need to see they are safe within a family unit, in which the grown-ups respect themselves enough to put their needs first. Not because parents are self-centered, but because they are the leaders and need to take care of themselves so the family can have happy guides who make safe and loving decisions that benefit everyone.

Make sure that, as a couple, you take time to be alone. You need private time in the sanctity of your bedroom and you need dinner dates and weekends that don't include the kids. You will teach your children a sense of personal autonomy as you demonstrate that the well-being of your marriage is essential.

My marriage comes first.

Children need to see Dad and Mom
having a life.

John and Linda Friel

Whether you have children, or are an influence to children around you, remember it's not what you say about life and love that counts in their learning and development, it's how you behave. Your marriage is not an isolated event. How you express feelings and the way you treat each other in public send ripple waves to all who are in your life . . . for good . . . or for not.

How we treat each other and our children is the groundwork for all of society. Make sure children see that Mommy and Daddy (or Auntie and Uncle) treat each other with respect, are affectionate with each other and demonstrate their concern for the well-being of the children. Loving well helps everyone.

Today, focus on the wide range of influence you have. Notice how many people see you with your spouse. Do they see you distant, bristling, miserable? Or do they see you holding hands and enjoying each other? What do you want your children to learn from the way you love?

**I show our children that love
and life are wonderful.**

❧

*The important gift you can give your children is the
knowledge that it is okay to be happy.*

Warren Beatty

L ooking back with regret, mentally whiplashing yourself for what you "should have done" gains you nothing. The event, the moment is over. You cannot go back and do it differently.

You can learn from the experience, of course, and that's what a wise person does. If you see that there might be a better way to receive praise, to make love, to approach a conflict, by all means take a moment to consciously decide that next time you'll do it differently. That is the adult, mature approach to learning from life. To pound on yourself puts you back into being a "bad child" and the punitive parent all at the same time.

Today, no matter what happens, pay attention to what is happening in the moment. The moment may even include a mutually respectful negotiation of a conflict. You may see your previous behavior with your spouse in a new light. But refuse to condemn yourself for the past.

**Today I will only focus on what's
right in front of me.**

*Should-haves solve nothing. It's the next thing to
happen that needs your thinking about.*

Alexandria Ripley

What's really happening when you say you are bored? If you think about it, you'll notice that *boredom* is the word we use to describe when we've disconnected from life. But, typically, we assume it's some outside person or event that is "boring." Yet, if we would enter more fully into the moment, no doubt we would find some way to be interested.

Boredom is the true opposite of love—the total absence of caring. When you catch yourself feeling bored, you can become curious about why you've withdrawn your love from the situation.

Even if you don't particularly like the person you're talking with at a party, or you know nothing about the topic your spouse is interested in, if you keep your heart open, you can ask questions that interest you, you can find ways to more fully enter into the experience instead of withdrawing into boredom. Don't be a bore!

I stay involved with life.

※

Somebody's boring me—
I think it's me.

Dylan Thomas

Perhaps misjudging our capabilities is the greatest "sin" we commit against ourselves. Sure, sometimes we expect far more than we could ever possibly accomplish and then condemn ourselves as failures. But far more often, it's the reverse. "I'm not pretty enough, he'll never ask me out." "I'm just an engineer, she probably wants a doctor." "Nobody will ever love me, I'm just fat and dumpy." We take ourselves out of the game without even trying.

We learned a lot of these self-condemning beliefs in early childhood. But as adults, let's use our minds and hearts to determine if they're really true. It's up to us to push past our preconceived, and very often false, limitations to find out what's really possible—in reality.

We all have limitations. That's part of being human. But don't use them against yourself. Otherwise you banish anything that exists out beyond your imagination—and there's lots more love and opportunity for you out there than you know!

I'm open to whatever's possible.

*Argue for your limitations,
and sure enough, they're yours.*

Richard Bach

E very day you make hundreds if not thousands of decisions, most of them on automatic pilot. The same old
routine day after day. As long as those decisions support
your health, well-being and personal dignity, so be it.

But too often we spend our entire day never once checking with our wise voice inside to see if we are really making
decisions that are right for us. When willing to be governed
by our past, hoping to get through the day as effortlessly as
possible, we never authentically encounter ourselves or our
lover. And then, what do we have to show for such mind-
lessness? Anything from boredom to loneliness, indigestion
and insomnia. Why? Because we've sold out our dignity.
We've sold out.

Today, practice making each and every decision consciously by asking this question: Is this in my best interest?
If not, it's not good for your relationship either. Then search
for a choice that dignifies your life and your love.

I listen to my inner voice to make my decisions.

❦

People attain worth and dignity by the multitude
of decisions they make from day to day.

Rollo May

So many people imagine when they're having relationship hassles, that if they just left and found someone new, it would be fine. What they don't realize is that similar problems would plague the next relationship as well, because they'd still be bringing their issues into the mix.

So why not stay with the one you're with and work it out where you are? You professed love to each other, at least in the beginning. You've stayed together however long it's been. You have a history. You have value for each other.

Yes, you've both been hurt by one another. You can learn to relate to each other with more respect and care, more compassion and forgiveness. Can you be forgiven, released to a more vulnerable surrender with your partner? Can you be forgiven and become lovable as you are? Can you receive the love you so dearly want, and save the relationship you have? If you open your heart just a little, what is your answer?

**I'll work it out with this spouse,
I don't want another.**

❧

*Many promising reconciliations have broken down because,
while both parties came prepared to forgive, neither
party came prepared to be forgiven.*

Charles Williams

Do you give money to charities? You probably do. But how about giving from the loving bond of your relationship? How could you offer hope to those who might benefit? What social causes really tug at your hearts? Where might the two of you want to contribute your time and your love?

Working together for a cause can be a very intimate and soul-satisfying activity, particularly if it opens you to deeper levels of vulnerability and gratitude. You may also open to love more willingly and more generously. Then, everyone benefits from your giving.

Take some time to fully discuss what kind of activities you both enjoy, and with which groups of people you would like to work. When you settle on a place or organization, remember that you are there as a loving couple to spread the gifts of the love you have achieved and to have your love regenerated by this blessed work of helping others.

It's fulfilling when we benefit our community.

※

Your love, given joyously to those in need,
can be more nourishing than bread.

Albert Niemiec

Many people get old before their time. Their love stagnates. Their bodies shut down. Their brains wither. Why? Because they've stopped being alive. They've stopped loving life. They've stopped learning.

Your mind is continually learning what you expect of it. If you feed it new ideas and new feelings, it loves to grow and expand. If you put it on a starvation diet, it will go into survival mode and that's it. Perhaps your mind gets a great workout every day, maybe not. But what if you developed a game the two of you could enjoy playing together that would, at the same time, keep your mind alert and expanding. Maybe a vocabulary game.

Each day you take turns picking a word out of the dictionary that neither of you uses or knows well. You teach it to your lover and then during the day you both make up sentences using the word, which you'll share later that night. Have fun! Your brain will thank you for loving it!

I enjoy playing games that help us learn.

We play vocabulary games on long drives and when we're out walking. It's great fun. We expand our awareness of language, the world and each other!

Helena S. Gertrudes

More and more people want a life that includes spiritual experience. They want life to hold more meaning. They want to experience the wisdom of their soul. They want to know God.

You are blessed. When used wisely, your relationship can provide the bridge between this material world and that of the divine. In fact, your soul is pulling you toward that bridge all the time. In many ways it is your soul that selected your mate, knowing you need the potent alchemical forces of your particular joining to move you into divine influence.

Every day, commit to becoming a truly conscious, compassionate human being. To help you do this, you are given the gift of romantic love. With your partner, aspire to an extraordinary love, a love of great passion and great fulfillment. Recognize that you are both seekers. Support each other in your search for the Larger Being within.

I notice the divine in my everyday life.

❧

Spirituality is a person's mystical quest to
experience the divine in their life.

Teresa M. Barton

154

Could you receive it if your spouse said, "You are the blessing of my life"? If so, congratulations! You know how much your very existence gives to your beloved. If you couldn't receive it, what's in the way? Distrust? Disbelief in your own value? Or honest awareness that you hold back who you are, giving very little to your spouse?

For love to flourish, you must make of yourself a blessing. Easier said than done, right? But you have to get beyond your self-protective fear. Otherwise love doesn't have a chance. Open yourself just a little bit more. Do you know he's afraid of your emotional distance? Does she feel insecure when you put yourself down?

Move toward your love just a little bit more. Be the blessing that you are. Consciously support your spouse. Be a force of praise. Feel love working its way with you. Offer yourself as a gift of love. You are a blessing. Know it. Share it. And most of all, receive it!

I give and receive the deep blessings of love.

Give the blessing of your support and your care.
Let your beloved know that in times
of difficulty you'll be there.

Edward Rudolph

Love means that you accept your partner as she is. But you also reserve the right to ask him to change. There is no such thing as purely unconditional love in a marriage. That would mean you never complain when your feelings are hurt, you never want anything except what is right in front of you. We humans are far more complex and spiritually ambitious than that. Thank God!

There are two important issues when you decide to ask for change. Make sure you're not trying to teach your lover to be a mirror of you. And don't waste your time requesting something that's outside the range of your lover's personality and character structure. There's no point in trying to mold your spouse into something she's not, and he'll buck and kick if he thinks only your way counts.

Asking for change is a fundamental aspect of intimacy and real romance. Asking with wisdom and respect is the sign of true love in action.

**I will only ask for important
and realistic change.**

❧

*Never try to teach a pig how to sing.
It wastes your time and annoys the pig.*

Source Unknown

156

We tend to think of making love as only sexual, in bed, with the lights dimmed. But if we relegate making love to just sex, we miss out on all the abundant opportunities there are to make love out of bed.

Don't burden sex with having to supply all the intimacy for your whole relationship. Keep intimacy and real romance a vital part of your everyday life together. Touch one another often—as you walk past each other, driving in the car, watching television, holding hands on the street, kissing anywhere. Enjoy giving and receiving compliments: They're just mini-love moments. Dance in the kitchen, shower together, give each other back rubs. Whatever you do, know that you are making love.

Use your imagination to give and receive love countless times a day. Be intimate. Be romantic. Be conscious that you are making love. Enjoy each other's special ways of making love—out of bed.

I enjoy making love out of bed.

∾

Making love can occur in so many small ways:
a special smile, a lingering touch … and sometimes
in giving your lover some space.

Laurie and Denny LeClear

Your differences hold so many levels of magic. Perhaps the most important and profound is that when you dig deep beneath the surface of any one of them, you will discover that you are essentially the same. You both hurt and you both want joy. You both desire freedom and meaningful fun. And you both want to be loved for all that you are.

When you get beyond the blinding shock of all the ways you're not the same, you discover the vast oneness that you also are.

In your rich humanity, the seeds of sameness wait for you. Meet one another in deep stillness and your two hearts will beat as one, for a time. And then you'll forget. Cluttered by the clamor of the world, you'll split apart. Divided. Longing to start the search for each other's deepest heart once again.

At bottom, we're the same.

❧

The more things look different, the more
they turn out to be the same.

K. C. Cole

You're growing, changing—and learning more about love than you ever could have imagined. Then why does your home look the same way it did when you first moved in together?

Celebrate yourselves: It's time to redecorate! Let your new love express itself in the way you live together. Maybe you don't have the time to do everything at once. Maybe the budget will only allow for a few minor tweaks. That's okay, as long as you consciously bring your new awareness of each other, and of life, into your physical surroundings.

You can start small. Humorous mouse pads. Sensuous sheets. Romantic toothbrush holder. Spiritual symbols. Your framed wedding picture hung in your bedroom. Or you can redo the whole place, making sure both of your tastes are represented, enjoying the process of discovering what you both like and dislike—and where your tastes collide but you want a dash of each other's "weirdness" in there to be sure to honor how different you are. When you're done, give yourselves a party!

I redecorate to reflect our changing love.

❧

If one changes internally, one should not continue to live with the same objects. They reflect one's mind and psyche of yesterday.

Anaïs Nin

Lots of people think that if they have sex after a fight, they've resolved their differences. But that's never the case. Oh, they may feel closer than before. They may be able to sleep through the night. But they are expecting healing powers from sex that sex can't offer. Only love can heal the wounds of a fight. Only love can keep the heart of your marriage together.

Sadly, lots of people think that hot, passionate sex is equivalent to love. It's not. It may accompany great love, but sex in itself is not love. One of the reasons for our astronomical divorce rate is the number of people who marry for lust rather than love.

Do not burden your sex life with the responsibility of keeping you together. Sex can be experienced in ways that enhance your love, certainly. But in itself, it can only be an attractor. You must create and nurture love every day if your marriage is going to be meaningful.

I don't rely on sex to hold us together.

❧

Passion, sexual passion, may lead to marriage,
but cannot sustain a marriage.

Edward Abbey

Now, it goes without saying that you are one of a kind. The question is, why do you work so hard at hiding the fact? It's so rare that you let yourself stand out in a crowd, or be the most confident one at the negotiating table. It's as if you think you're supposed to just blend in instead of flaunting your stuff. What's the deal?

It's your life after all! Why not live it for all that it's worth? Develop your own unique dress style. Cultivate a business presence that keeps all eyes on you. Speak up with your controversial opinions. Be a leader in your community. Give fabulous low-budget parties with a focus on really meaningful conversation. Whatever you do, be creative and inventive.

Too bold, you say? Too brash? Nah. Just trying to get you to paint yourself—God's creation—with a broader brush. God will have more fun and so will you!

I emphasize my differences with joy and grace.

If you're not different, you're gonna lose.

Eminem

M ost of us have learned to take ourselves *sooooo* seriously. We act as if everyone is watching to see us make a mistake, to make fun of us if we step out of line just one little bit. Whew! What a heavy psychic burden to carry around.

But what if you knew that everyone else—everyone— had the same concerns, and you could see how absurd that was? What if you saw that tiptoeing around in life, afraid of everyone else's judgment, was like selling your soul to the devil? What if that woke you up so completely that you stopped taking yourself so seriously? Can you feel the freedom that would open up? Can you see how love might feel far more welcome to visit?

By all means, be serious about the choices you make and how you treat others, most especially your lover. But relax about the uptight stuff you learned ages ago.

I relax and accept myself.

≈

Don't take yourself seriously.
Take what you do seriously and find the
humor in as much of life as you can.

Ben Affleck

God created us in his/her own image, so it is said. Yet many of us persist in imagining that God is in heaven, separated and apart from us. But if God created us, then what are we if not each an aspect of God?

Does this sound blasphemous? In certain beliefs, the answer is "Yes!" But not in all. So, you get to choose. Would you rather evolve your own sense of God or blindly follow someone else's? Either way it's up to you. Remember, God created you to be a creator also.

If you really take it in that you are a manifestation of God, how does that impact the way you live? The way you love? The way you receive love? The way you create your life? God needs you to recognize that part of reality that is God. What part? The part that is you, that is God.

I see God in everyone.

❧

People see God every day.
They just don't recognize him.

Pearl Bailey

Your relationship is an ongoing invention, a collaboration between the two of you, the unique combining of your two personalities, interests, life goals and much more. Even if certain aspects are preset by your church or gender or culture, the rest will be your own collaborative invention.

You must get to know each other, and continue to do so to invent your own intimacy. You will also continually decide what you tell each other. Some couples tell each other everything, other couples prefer not to know about each other's pasts or the daily gossip from the workplace. Each couple invents their own brand of honesty, specific to their joined temperaments and the level of intimacy they desire.

Today, consciously invent how you will put yourself forward with a focus on honesty—what you will say and what you won't. Notice the impression your choice makes on your spouse. Notice to what degree you invent your self-image as open and forthcoming, and to what degree you hold back.

I'm inventive as we co-create our love.

*Just as every couple has to invent sex for itself,
it also has to invent honesty.*

Adam Phillips

Y ou may feel baffled by events in your life. You may feel like a victim, as if everything is conspiring against you. But that idea will just victimize you. In fact, it can push you to unconsciously act out abusively at your spouse. Don't do that.

Instead, look to events in your life as spiritual teachers. Even if it's hard to believe, examine them as if there are no accidents. What do you notice if you accept that everything happens for a reason? Do you begin to see patterns emerge? How do you make choices that eventually lead to pain—or pleasure? What are you doing?

Read your life like a good novel. There is a main plot and lots of subplots. What are yours? If you want to change the story, change your choices. Then look for seemingly "out of the blue" events. Perhaps they'll be part of a new, more exciting love story.

I open to the deeper meanings.

❧

There are no random events.
Look for the deeper meaning to see how love is working
in you, conspiring to support your growth,
urging you to love better.

Carolyn Ranker

June

*When Chris and I got married
we'd been together five years and we
were very clear we wanted to be married
for better or worse. It's very hard to
believe we've been together ten years,
because we're still so in love.
It's nice to honestly feel I have no regrets.
Would I change who I married?
Never.*

DANA REEVE
(WIFE OF CHRISTOPHER REEVE)

When you're not fully committed to your marriage, you will always be able to find reasons to leave. Why? Because you've got a backdoor escape route, so you'll always be able to find an excuse to exit. But if you do, you'll just be attracted to someone much like your current partner and then be in the same predicament all over again. Why? Because you're wired to be attracted in the same way so you'll get what you now have.

Why not continue to learn the very many reasons there are to stay together? When he's late, you get to practice asking for more consideration and you can learn to be more patient. When she's controlling, you get to learn how to be better organized and how to help her become more relaxed. When you're both committed to making it work, then everything that happens is another lesson in mature love.

Lifelong marriage is a daily meditation on the practical spirituality of love. You must choose, each day, to find the blessings and to grow together.

Every day I find grounds to continue my marriage.

In every marriage more than a week old,
there are grounds for divorce. The trick is to find, and
continue to find, grounds for a marriage.

Robert Anderson

How do you feel about your spouse? Really? Okay, you love him, you adore her. Now get more specific. What really excites you about the one you married? How do you celebrate the feelings you have when you see each other after a long separation? When you make love, what thrills you about being with this special person? Do you think about these questions? Or do you just accept that you love your spouse, and that's that?

Don't miss the joy of enjoying the very particular ways your spouse is a treat to be with, all the yummy ways your sweetheart turns you on sexually. It's up to you to notice and to feel the ecstatic feelings enjoyment breeds.

You are the creator of your joy. It is from you that your spouse is given the specialness that you perceive. And it is you that chooses to enjoy your spouse's company in ways no one else could ever imagine!

I find deep joy with my spouse.

To have joy in another is love.

Karl Barth

170

Sometimes it's not much fun being a grown-up. Go to work. Clean the house. Take care of the kids. Pay the bills. Remember someone's birthday . . . and on and on. . . .

Okay, you do have to do all that stuff, but you can also have more fun. Set aside some times to just be silly. Act like kids. You can have water-pistol fights, fly a kite, finger paint. Go to your local children's museum and join in. Rent some cartoons, pop popcorn, make sure to have your favorite candy and spend an evening being ten-year-olds again. Make a feast and eat with your hands. Visit the arcade and play some of the games. Go to the children's zoo and pet the animals—take photos of how cute you both are with the baby animals!

Every so often, indulge your inner kids! Give them lots of freedom to express themselves and offer your adults some rowdy fun. Be sure to enjoy each other's version of being a kid!

I will be more playful.

If you think life has become a bit too serious recently,
toss your worries aside and act like a kid.

Michael Webb

Remember when you were dating and had to have a steady stream of chatter to know that things were going okay? If there was even a pause in the conversation, one of you would rush in and fill it up, to make sure neither of you would have to feel anxious. Quite a strain, right?

Well, now that you're settled in with your sweetheart, do you allow for the beauty of silence to surround you? If so, how well do you enjoy the quiet space? How well do you trust your love to linger and live in the silence? If you have trouble allowing silence to contain you, what's going on? What's the anxiety about?

The trust of silence in love makes for many magical moments that could not occur with the onrush of voices. Entwined euphoria after making love. Spellbound awe at nature's wonders. Deep relaxation at the beach, by a lake. The comfort of a lasting hug. The bliss of falling asleep holding hands. Silence is more than golden, it is the voice of your deep trust and comfort.

I love the silence of love.

⤬

Love is when you stop saying nonsense things
and can simply be silent.

Kaitlin Rogers

When you were younger you no doubt thought that Grumpy belonged with Snow White, not in your marriage. Now you know differently. It's impossible to meet the disappointments of everyday life as well as the tensions in your marriage without occasionally becoming grumpy. That's just life.

The tragedy is that so many people don't realize that the freedom to be grumpy with one another is a very intimate form of romance. Not the funnest side of romance, no doubt about that—but an aspect of real romance that can elicit deep compassion and closeness, when you keep your heart open to the entirety of love.

The freedom to be all that you are—even grumpy, self-centered and unshaven from time to time (for both of you)—is one of the deepest blessings of love. It's not always pleasant, even annoying. But when you love each other even when you're grumpy, then it's a love you know is true. Grump, grump!

Real romance includes being grumpy.

I finally figured out who all the grumpy,
selfish, impatient lovers are.
They're all of us, and we all take turns.

Jack Kammer

Even if you're not married, you already have at least a couple of anniversaries you can celebrate—the day you met and your first date. If you're married, there's the date you got engaged and of course your wedding date. Then there are the major milestones you've experienced together—the day your dog joined the family, the day you purchased your first house, opened a business together. . . .

Celebrate your life together. Honor one another and the life you've created by inventing special ways to observe your "Love Days." For example, on the anniversary of your first date you might replicate it as much as possible. Go to the same restaurant or movie theater, or give a party similar to the one you attended. On your wedding anniversary you might look through your wedding photos and then go to a nice hotel for a romantic night.

Celebrate yourselves as often as possible. It's fun. It's romantic. And it helps deepen the special, private intimacy the two of you share.

I celebrate all our important anniversaries.

⚜

Now we celebrate our anniversary monthly . . .
and we have a better relationship.

Dan McKenzie

You can stop wishing that your spouse was more like you. The fact is some of those differences are hard-wired in the brain.

In the last couple of decades scientific research has proven that males and females think differently. They process information differently, because their brains are shaped and organized differently. The biggest differences are in the areas of the brain that handle spatial processes—the ability to picture things in the mind's eye. Hundreds of studies demonstrate that men's brains have better spatial ability. That's why men can read maps better than women. On the other hand, women can read people's character better. Men's eyes are better shaped for tunnel vision and women's for peripheral vision, and on and on.

The biological differences are here to stay. So let's make use of each other's expertise to enhance our lives together. Appreciate the differences!

I will remember we are biologically different.

The sexes are different because their
brains are different.

Anne Moir and David Jessel

175

To have known great love and lose the person you love may be the most searing loss one can endure. To share a deep, sacred passion and have to be apart for great lengths of time can also be quite difficult. Either way, the question is: How do you cope? How do you make the most of life and love?

If your spouse leaves through death, it may seem difficult to believe you could love again. Yet, to love again is the miracle made possible by having known true love. For once you know the sacred magic of love, no pain can ever prevent you from loving again. On the other hand, if you must be apart from one another for some time, so long as you carry each other in your hearts, the power of love will sustain you.

Remember, it is in the love you carry, heart and soul, that you are sustained and made whole, over and over again.

The love that lives in my heart makes me whole.

❦

I understand how a man who has
nothing left in this world may still blow a kiss…
in the contemplation of his beloved.

Viktor Frankl

What is the highest spiritual purpose for marriage? What if marriage can be the spiritual incubator for your personal greatness? Or does that just sound like psychobabble? Well, from a spiritual point of view, the best way you can love your God is to make the very most out of what has been given to you.

When two people join their lives together, there are the issues of livelihood and homemaking. But there is the larger issue of who you could be if you expressed your greatness. That's a challenge from the soul. That's the invitation to follow spirit. When a married couple supports one another in following their paths to greatness, they engage in a spiritual adventure, a profoundly practical form of loving God.

Make a date with your spouse to imagine and define your individual paths to greatness. Then support each other in following these paths to even greater love—of God, yourselves and each other.

I support both of us becoming great.

Keep away from people who try to belittle your ambitions.
Small people do that. The really great make you feel
that you, too, can become great.

Mark Twain

K issing. There are so many ways to kiss. And so many reasons to kiss. And it feels so good! Then why, after we've been with someone for awhile, do we allow kissing to get relegated to sexual foreplay and/or habitual greetings?

You can kiss passionately while waiting for the pasta to cook or the eggs to boil. You can leave a kiss on the top of the head when he's sitting at the computer. Kiss her hand while waiting for the light to turn green. Kiss him all over to wake him up. Send a kiss balloon to her office. Blow kisses to say good-bye. Leave a sloppy one and then play hide-and-go-seek. Plant a lipstick kiss on his mirror. Kiss the back of her knee when you're at the beach. Kiss tenderly before saying good-night.

From heavy breathing to pecks on the cheek, kissing is a very romantic way to say "I love you" many times throughout the day. Do it often!

I will take every opportunity to kiss . . . yummmm!

❧

When you kiss, your mouth produces more saliva,
which helps prevent tooth decay.

Academy of General Dentistry

It's so easy to compare yourself with others, putting yourself down. They are more—more caring, generous, popular, successful, more . . . something. And they may be. But that has nothing to do with your life, your challenges and your triumphs—with your unique capacity to love.

You came into this life with particular gifts and limitations. No one else will ever know what it has taken for you to risk your heart and soul the way you do, not even your dear spouse. Because no one will have ever lived inside your skin except you. Your way of loving is a miracle. It will be lost—for all time—if you hold back because your way is different. Don't do it.

Comparisons waste your energy and take your focus off what you can do today to become more open. Envy robs you of your own passion. Remember, all you can do is live your desire, follow your dream and put the very best you have out into the world.

My journey can't be compared with anyone else's.

Resist the temptation to compare yourself to others.
You have to really watch out for the idea
that what other people have means that
you haven't been fairly treated.

Wayne Dyer

How often do you consciously use music to convey your love? No doubt you enjoy music together. But what about using music to make love? Not just in the background when you're having sex, but to actually express love.

Use music to express the deepest aspects of your passion. Play a song that reveals the voice of your spirit as a way to be very intimate and vulnerable. Surprise your lover with a piece that portrays a unique aspect of her. Play a tune of repentance to apologize to him. Speak to each other of love through music. Be available to listen with your hearts, to hear one another's spirits in the music.

When you make love through music, you can consciously choose what you'll play when you're soaking in the tub together or having sex—and know it's not just beautiful music. It's also "I love you."

I enhance our romance through music.

We can touch one another's hearts through music.
Sharing music is joy, freedom and prayer.

Johar Coleman

How often we betray love with our fears and doubts that say "No" when we mean "Yes." We wait, hoping we have the occasion again to say yes, but life keeps on going by and then we say no because we're mad—but wish we'd said yes.

Yes can be magical. If we would but give yes more of a chance in our lives, no could come with more self-respect, instead of pout and sulk. Try yes more often, trusting that even nervousness can be soothed by yes. Embolden no for when you really need it by planting yes into the heart of love. Fear not the yes that succumbs to favorite charms, for its stance on your behalf can only please you.

Say yes all your days and play out the ardor of your love, for yes, oh yes, yes, say yes.

I say "yes" to love and life.

...yes and his heart was going like mad
and yes I said yes I will Yes.

James Joyce

Some people say "No" all the time in their marriage and seldom mean it. They threaten and they rant, shouting no, no, no. But they never leave and their word counts for nought. Others seldom say no, but their silence deals the blow.

One of the major complaints men and women have against one another is that they don't know where they stand. Yes means no. No means yes. Wiles and beguiles pass for truth while the truth gets lost behind the rules. The goal for your no is to know you mean no.

When you use no, mean it. Not just sort of. But absolutely. That doesn't mean you can't change your mind. But to say no with so much guilt and shame that your partner feels the blame, that's not a fair game. Play for freedom. Even if your spouse wants sex and you don't, a false yes just comes out flat. Don't cheat your marriage by cheating on NO.

I will say no when I mean it and I'll mean it.

*I must say . . . a fast word about oral contraception.
I asked a girl to go to bed with
me and she said "no."*

Woody Allen

Y̧ou never just marry another person. You always acquire in-laws as well. Not to mention the conversion your own parents and family make as they too become in-laws. Even if parents are dead, their influence will color your marriage forever.

Right from the beginning, you are teaching your parents and in-laws how they can treat you and what they can expect from your marriage. Unless you want to wreck your marriage, don't allow them to treat you like children. Yes, you're a son and daughter, but you are not children. Don't take your marital problems to them and don't give them the key to your house. Insist they treat you both with respect and insist that they not impose their values on you.

Your marriage must be protected from any interference or invasion by in-laws—any of them. Draw up "Rules of the House" for all of your relatives. Make sure you both agree to them and are prepared to enforce them. Change them as needed. Be adults!

I insist our parents respect us as grown-ups.

❧

Tell [your mother] in no uncertain terms that the fact that she and your father have paid for the wedding does not entitle her to a copy of your gift list, nor access to your personal financial information. You must draw the line now.

Abigail Van Buren (Dear Abby)

What do you consider to be the treasure at the heart of your relationship? Your money? You could lose it all. Your children? They'll grow up and leave you. What about all the ways you risk yourselves with each other? All the hurts and slights that you take to one another to be comforted and healed. All the problems you share and fix together. What if those are the real wealth of your love?

You see, each time you need one another's help and receive it, you add more value to your marriage. Every time you face a tragedy or problem together you forge a deeper connection. The more you learn to trust one another with the fragile experiences of life, the more beautiful is your inner tapestry. The stuff we most like to withhold is the most precious of love's wealth.

Make an interest payment to your spouse by sharing your richest memories of being cared for, helped and healed by the blessings of love.

**I will invest more of myself into
the value of my marriage.**

*Love comes gradually with our worry, relief and care—
with what we have invested of ourselves.*

Frances Karlen Santamaria

The vulnerability of intimacy leaves you wide open to being wounded, even when your lover's words sound wonderful. Words are never pure unto themselves because they're delivered by a tone of voice. The words may even seem admiring, but then you hear something in the delivery. You may not even know what you are reacting to, but you no longer feel safe.

In order to trust one another more deeply, you need to learn when your verbal expressions rub the wrong way. "I was just joking" or "You're just too sensitive" or "How could you have thought that about me" are all good reasons for suspicion that there's more to the message than meets the eye.

You must learn to hear your own delivery, and aim to have your tone of voice match your words. So today, observe your tone of voice. Learn to hear the edge that belies your irritation, the leaking contempt. Look for the full, graceful tones that carry your love across with complete clarity.

I notice not just my words but my tone of voice.

The way you say a thing is part of what you say,
so you have to choose the right way.

Isabel Bishop

Most people get married without ever talking about the real-world stuff of a marriage: how to handle money, how they'll share child-rearing and housework, and—most importantly—their life goals. In other words, they unite their lives "till death us do part" without a road map or blueprint for where they're going. Then they fight about their differing impulses and needs until they end up in divorce court.

Every serious venture of our lives needs a plan. People make up business plans, lesson plans and plans for emergency evacuation, but sadly too many of us never bother to define our life plan: the purpose and goals for our future together and the direction of our marriage.

Today, make a date with your spouse to develop a life plan together. Spend the day thinking about what you want to accomplish together, within your family and in the world. Let the plan you jointly design guide your life choices and the expression of your love.

I will help us organize a life plan.

The vital, successful people I have met all had one common characteristic. They had a plan.

Marilyn Van Derbur

Turn off the TV, the video games, the Internet. Be with each other. Be with each other in the silence, if you have to, just to discover what else you might want to do together. The intensity between you may be astonishing. The shyness and embarrassment may be shocking. But what's a marriage for, if not to wake you up from time to time?

If you have children, they will love having more of your attention. You can read to them. If they are older, each of you can take turns reading some book out loud, followed by popcorn and a discussion about what you've just read. If it's just the two of you, it's a wonderful opportunity to explore your discomfort with each other, or to go dancing, play pool, go bowling, make cookies, anything that brings you together.

Turn off your TV and turn on your love. It's as simple as that. Will you do it?

I choose love instead of TV.

We were amazed at the way TV had truncated our ability to converse.... It cheers me to see how much closer our family has grown now that the loudest, most disruptive voice in the house is under our control.

Emily Prager

Every couple has a history. Both people can remember times when they felt hurt or betrayed by the other. If these old issues have never been resolved and you hang on to them to justify your distance and lack of intimacy, you're creating your own emotional hell.

Work through the difficult times as they come up. If there is still old stuff separating you, make a date to begin the healing process, perhaps with the help of a counselor. The future of your love cannot be opened as long as you cling to the wounds of the past. You may be afraid to try again, to make yourself vulnerable, to trust that true intimacy can be yours. That's understandable. Yet, you can either be miserable for life, or start anew with a commitment to opening your heart to mature love.

Start your future today. When thoughts of the past arise, stop them and refocus on what you can do to give birth to a new aspect of your relationship.

I will leave the past behind.

❧

What is done is done.

Shakespeare, *Macbeth*

You may think that adult awareness and understanding of love just come with age, with being an adult over twenty-one or twenty-five or even fifty. But look around you. It's not true. Most people still love like emotionally terrified teenagers or needy, grabby children, no matter their age.

Adult loving must be developed. Happily, the process of becoming an adult requires the same awareness and emotional skills as mature love. So, when you decide to grow up, you can use any of life's experiences to support your developing maturity and deepening intimacy. The hallmark of mature adulthood is your ability to respect your own unique reality and that of your spouse. You must be able to hold two realities at the same time, negotiating a third different reality together when necessary or desirable.

To the best of your ability, make sure you are approaching your loving as an adult today. Think of your own needs, and think of your spouse's needs with equal weight. Commit yourself to the well-being of both of you.

I will love as an adult.

~

We might say that adulthood has been "discovered" in this age in the same way that childhood was the discovery of the seventeenth century and adolescence of the late nineteenth.

Lillian B. Rubin

No matter how much you change and grow on your own, certain key elements of personal transformation can only occur in the alchemical fire of romantic love. Why? Because it's only the vulnerability and intensity of deep emotional intimacy that can trigger your innermost issues. Only by the heat and pressure of passionately committed love will you be transformed into a glorious celebration of all that you are.

Don't dance on the surface of love! That's boring. That kills love. Fling yourself open to the passions that arise, no matter how dark, how terrorizingly beautiful. You were created in rich complexity, which you learned to hide from the insensitive and the cruel. It's understandable. But now, face to face with love, don't waste another minute making less of yourself.

Walk into the transformational power of love. Yes, sometimes it will be painful, sometimes frightening. Sometimes ecstatic! And what do you get? Greater and greater awareness of your God-given magnificence, as well as a richer, more robust and magical love!

I am being transformed by our love.

❧

A clay pot sitting in the sun will always be a clay pot.
It has to go through the white heat of the
furnace to become porcelain.

Mildred Witte Stouven

Have you ever thought about the overarching purpose for marriage? For marital commitment? Yes, it's wonderful to have companionship, great sex, children perhaps. But what about developing yourselves together? How about creating your own mature status in the world with each other's support? Have you considered that you could heal old emotional wounds through your loving experiences together?

When you understand that marriage is meant to be a learning experience, it will make it much easier to accept the lessons love has for you. They are inevitable because you are different from each other. Your different points of view are bound to open new vistas, new meanings for one another. Without them you would never mature, you would never be able to deepen your knowing of one another.

What are the lessons of your love today? No matter what happens between you, consider how you can use the experience to learn more about yourself and your spouse.

Anything in our life can be my teacher.

Everything that happens is either a blessing which is also a lesson, or a lesson which is also a blessing.

Polly Berrien Berends

A physical rush may announce your initial attraction. You may get a gut feeling that "this is the Right One." Those early instinctual knowings are merely early signs that something serious might be possible with this particular person.

Once you are both interested in exploring a potential future together, a great deal of what will happen depends on how available each of you is to the process of creating a loving relationship. To the degree that you are emotionally and spiritually generous with your attraction, care and compassion, the more you will be able to give to your partner your belief that he or she is worthy of your abiding love. To the degree that you are suspicious, lost in fantasy, needful of control—the less this can happen.

Notice today that you are the creator of each moment's involvement with your spouse. You can either approach with kindness, compassion and goodwill or not. It is always your choice.

Conscious love is more important than instinct.

Love is not an instinct, but rather a creation.

José Ortega y Gasset

Modern science teaches us that a loving relationship is very good medicine. A woman who has her beloved spouse with her during childbirth has an easier, less painful experience. Having music you love or your favorite flowers in your hospital room speeds up your recovery. So, if you live with someone who loves you dearly, how does that affect your overall health?

Well, your body loves it when you experience the warmth and security of being loved. It relaxes. It fills up on revitalizing hormones and other good biochemistry. It thrives on this healthy, loving environment, giving you good energy, strengthening your immune system and adding to your longevity. You feel great.

Make your home a haven of health. Create a tribute to your mutual health by cooking and eating delicious, fun and healthy food. The more you focus on being healthy, the more you love yourself. The more you receive love and the more you give it, the healthier you are. To your health!

My body and my health are blessed by our love.

❧

We are proving that love is part of our physiology,
that our feelings manifest in our body.

Bernie Siegel

Anger and conflict are sure to arise in any marriage based on a commitment to love. Fighting for the health and growth of your love and the liveliness of you both is like good fertilizer: It may smell and be sort of messy, but it helps you grow your intimacy ever deeper and richer.

But for most couples, fights are repetitious—the kind that surface over and over and never get resolved. Since they don't know how to fight for their love, each of them fights to win! Then they fall into deadly power struggles. Both people are just making sure they don't lose. All that does is destroy love.

You need a method that will get you past the repetition. You can reconceive conflict and make it your ally. After all, a conflict is like an SOS signaling the need for change. Heed it well, so that when it arises, it's a way of fighting for your relationship rather than against your partner.

**I'll fight for our well-being,
rather than just try to win.**

❦

*If you continue to do what you've always done,
you're going to get what you always got.*

Source Unknown

When you're in public, wouldn't it be great to have a private way to signal each other, "I love you," or "I want to leave," or "Help, rescue me from this conversation!"? Well, you can. Just make up your own personal signals.

You could use three of anything to mean "I love you"—three taps on his arm, three candies on her chair, even three Post-It notes on the dashboard or windshield. Or you could decide together that rubbing your nose means "I want to leave." Putting both hands on your cheeks could call out, "Help, rescue me from this conversation." There's no limit to the signal messages that might be meaningful and useful to you both.

Not only does your personal sign language help you function better, more gracefully in public, but it also connects you in a bold, private affirmation of your special love.

**Our own private sign language
can be very romantic.**

❧

*The marvelous richness of human experience
would lose something of rewarding joy if there
were no limitations to overcome.*

Helen Keller

How often do you cheat on your marriage by not making time for it? Many people do that. They find time for their children, their parents, their career, housework, working out, but not lovework. Why do you suppose that is? What do you get to avoid by making other things more important than the love of your life?

The answer for most people, if they are really honest, is that they're nervous about being emotionally intimate. They don't know how to receive love very well. They have difficulty speaking clearly about what they'd like—and then receiving the gift of love when their request is met with "Yes." So it's less stressful to do something that's familiar, that will take up a lot of time and prohibit intimacy.

Don't cheat yourself by making the excuse that you "don't have the time" for love. Of course you do—if it's your priority. And what else could possibly be more important than making time for love?

I commit to making time for my marriage.

❧

You will never "find" time for anything.
If you want time, you must make it.

Charles Buxton

Love and life are never all-the-time bubbly and fascinating. Sometimes your marriage seems to grind to a dull halt. Love seems limp and flat. Yuck! What a drag! What is happening?

Yes, on the surface love seems to have disappeared. Your marriage may even seem like it's over. But do not despair. Your marriage is in drydock being scraped of barnacles and other hard things. Love is at low ebb. It may feel boring. That's why it's so important to know that you have a life of your own and can fish off the pier while you wait for love to float your boat again.

When love dries up, so to speak, it's usually a time of integration. You've been doing some lovework, things have been getting even better and then, wham! But love is growing, deep in the ocean of your souls. Trust yourselves and trust your love. The sails will catch the wind once again, and it will be more glorious sailing than ever before.

I am committed to love even when it's on hold.

Love winter when the plant says nothing.

Thomas Merton

Whether you stay at home or go outdoors, mealtime offers great opportunities to make love out of bed. Rather than just do the habitual meal thing in front of the TV or even at the dining table, try some new ways to enjoy eating together.

Try eating in different places. If you take your lunch or dinner to another room—or to a pretty place in your yard, a nearby park, close by a body of water or even near a railroad track—it opens a fresh dimension on being together and enjoying more of what is in your world.

Add to that your favorite foods, easy-to-wash tablecloth and napkins, attractive nonbreakable dishes and glasses, *Voila*! A romantic feast.

Open yourselves to the new experience. Don't just move the feast and then munch as usual. The point is to become more aware of how new surroundings open you to a different perspective on your love and your life together. *Salud!*

I will make mealtime romantic.

We can make a simple meal into a celebration
of life when we go outdoors and settle into a favorite
spot that connects us back to nature.

Art Klein and Pat Feinman

July

*Burn, burn, burn like
fabulous yellow Roman candles
exploding like spiders across the stars
and in the middle you see the blue
centerlight pop and everybody
goes "Awwwww!"*

JACK KEROUAC

The Bible suggests that God will come again and he/she will bring fire. Some believe the fire will destroy the Earth. But what if the Fire of Love is evidence of God's presence on Earth, destroying all that is not of love? Not so far-fetched, right? And much more plausible than a God who wants to destroy all that he/she created.

However you think about this, your willingness to open your heart more fully, to love more intensely, is no minor matter. Consider that your ability to love is a powerful force far beyond your personal life and marriage. Your choice to ignite an ever-burning Fire of Love in your heart helps over-turn the hell of hatred and fear of differences that perpetu-ate prejudice and violence in society.

God is love. To know God, and be evidence of God's abundance on Earth, let the fire of love continually burn through you.

The fire of love teaches me about the divine.

The day will come when, after harnessing the ether,
the winds, the tides, and gravitation, we shall harness for God
the energies of love. And, on that day, for the second time in
the history of the world, man will have discovered fire.

Pierre Teilhard de Chardin

N o one is born with self-confidence. It is always earned and developed by overcoming adversity or rising to a challenge. If you want stronger self-confidence, it will have to be an inside job. Your lover can't give it to you. Not even love can give it to you.

But love can supply the challenges. That's the beauty of love: it has just what you need to develop yourself. Start by listing all the things you find difficult in your relationship—difficult for you to do. For example: asking for help, exchanging gifts, debating politics, taking time for yourself, spending money on yourself, disagreeing with his parents, standing up to her child by a previous marriage. Across from each issue, describe what you need to do differently that would build your self-confidence.

You've just designed your own workout program—guaranteed to build your self-confidence muscle—provided that you make the changes you just listed. Push through the anxiety. You'll be very glad you did!

I courageously develop self-confidence.

Physical beauty is ephemeral, but the self-confidence one builds from achieving difficult things and accomplishing goals is the most beautiful thing of all.

Madonna

L ife is what you make it. And you either make it heaven or you make it hell. Pretty awesome choice, right? But it's true, and it's up to you.

No one is saying this choice is easy. But it is simple. You either choose love or you don't. Either way, your path will be filled with challenges. If you choose love, all the internal barriers to love will come to the surface to be healed. If you don't choose love, every misery you own will surface crying out to be loved. Either way, the forces of heaven are out to claim your soul. You can either surrender and learn how to love better or resist and suffer all the way. You choose.

Here's the guarantee. To the degree that you can surrender to love, you will know heaven on Earth. To the degree that you refuse love, your life will be a living hell, every day. Choose!

I am responsible for choosing heaven on Earth.

❦

There is only one path to heaven.
On Earth, we call it love.

Karen Goldman

I s your marriage your primary family? Or is your first loyalty to your parents? For your marriage to flourish, you must make your spouse the most important person in your life, second only to yourself. You may feel guilt just thinking of leaving home, freeing yourself from being your parents' obedient boy or girl. Of course, you'll always be their son or daughter, but you must leave your past behind and now love them adult to adult.

You can love your parents, or their memory, with all your heart and soul. But you cannot remain their "child" and create a wonderful marriage. You must choose. And what could be a better day to do this than Independence Day, when we celebrate leaving Mother England behind?

Take stock of the ways you're not fully committed to your partner. Your primary allegiance might be parents, your children, your job, anything. Today, choose to put your marriage first. Celebrate your independence and your marriage!

I celebrate my independence and maturity.

❦

You can be up to your boobies in white satin,
with gardenias in your hair and no sugarcane for miles,
but you can still be working on a plantation.

Billie Holiday

L ife can be very harsh. You can get broadsided by the loss of a job, a failed investment, a brutal disease. These are times when you desperately need each other, and you must offer and receive as much comfort as possible. But what else can you do to sustain yourselves?

Many people turn to art—other people's or their own. You may be thinking you're an artistic clod. You feel overwhelmed in museums and put off by the snotty salespeople in art galleries. Art-schmart.

But art can move you out of yourselves, at least for a short time, and bring you a taste of transcendence. Whether you gaze on a masterpiece or a local painting at a craft fair, you can let your consciousness enter the piece and find a new perspective. Making art yourself can likewise help you express your feelings and move you through pain into new awareness. Let art do its part in helping you both cope with the bad times.

I will remember there can be comfort in art.

When life fails you, art can be a salvation.

Kelsey Grammer

Buried inside each of us is an artist waiting to be invited out. Unfortunately, most of the time this closeted artist takes itself way too seriously. "Why paint if I can't make money from it?" "No one else would understand my strange novel!" "Wood carving, a thing of the past!" But the internal artist yearns to follow its imagination, to fly in free expression. Just for the fun of it.

Give each other permission to be creative. It doesn't matter whether it's writing, music, whatever. Don't worry about being any good. Being good isn't the point. Playing with your imagination and expressing your impulses, your vision—that's the point.

Make dates to enjoy creative playtime together. You could take classes at your local night school. Or just set up a space at home to let the Muse speak through you. Enjoy each other's courage and talent. Feel the romance of playing in your own private imaginarium.

I am enriched by our creative playtime.

∞

Imagination is the highest kite that can fly.

Lauren Bacall

E ven if you both grew up in the same town, with the same ethnic background and same religion, you still grew up with cultural differences: your different family cultures. But if you marry someone who comes from a different country, different ethnic background, with different language and different religion, cultural differences are going to be dramatic.

Cross-cultural differences are simply invitations to see the world through differing value systems, differing philosophies, differing visions of God. To love one another and share your distinct cultural perspectives, you must allow yourself to be humbled by the strength and beauty of these long-lasting societies and civilizations.

When you marry across cultures, you sit at the altar of God's mosaic. As long as your hearts are open to one another, you can sift through your differences in order to worship the mosaic in a new way—your own co-created way!

I am enriched by our cultural differences.

When I try to get complex, it confounds her.
She smiles, and in the simplicity of her
response, I recognize another way.

Justin Weiner
(American-born, lives in Thailand
with his love, Amphon)

You can experience fierce passions in response to the one you love. As fierce as sexual heat can drive you, so too can wild hatred fired in a flash of anger born of hurt and fear. Hatred is not the opposite of love, indifference is.

A burst of hate is usually a momentary eruption, a rage against the gods. However, hatred held over time is emotional disturbance that needs professional care.

Don't be surprised if you feel flashes of hatred for your lover. But don't act out physically or by calling names, wanting to hurt your lover's feelings. You may want to talk about your feelings, knowing they are momentary, and, no doubt, in large measure an expression of old hurts and fears triggered by what's happening in the moment. Your lover can learn about your wounds and better understand the intense feelings they generate. That's how the depths of hatred can lead to the heights of love.

I understand that I can hate the one I love.

*I love her and she loves me, and we hate each other
with a wild hatred born of love.*

August Strindberg

The capacity to enjoy life depends on your ability to love. The more you love, the more you can value life. To the degree that you hold back from love, you hold back from life. It's that simple.

The mere act of opening your heart to another may be the greatest triumph of your life. In fact, growing up, you may have been made fun of if you were overly tender or sensitive. So you may have closed yourself off. And now as an adult you are working to gain back the wonder of your spirit.

Each of us must remember that we have no idea how anyone else was raised, what they may have had to endure in the name of love. So, the greatest gift we can give anyone is our commitment to love them for who they are. Just that.

I put love at the center of my life.

❧

Love doesn't make the world go 'round, love is what makes the ride worthwhile.

Shirley Taylor Haizlip and
Harold C. Haizlip

There is no such thing as being powerless in a relationship. Even if it feels that way, you are always having an impact on your spouse and on your relationship. You can be assertive. You can be submissive. Either way you are impacting what can and what can't happen between the two of you.

Ironically, it's the person who holds back the most that has the most power in the relationship. The other person can plead, beg, flip cartwheels trying to get things onto a new, more intimate track, but if you won't budge—who wins? You do. But what do you win, really?

Just the power struggle, that's all. Certainly you both lose at love.

Pay attention to all the ways you impact your spouse today. Be affectionate and notice your impact. Be distracted by work and notice how you're impacting the routine you share or how you interrupt a social plan. Notice your impact all day. And notice how it feels to be powerful.

I recognize my impact.

If you think you're too small to have an impact,
try going to bed with a mosquito.

Anita Koddick

D o you worry that you're not attractive enough to keep your spouse's attraction and passion? Do you wish you looked like Sharon Stone or Sean Connery? Well, stop wasting time doubting yourself. Certainly, it's important that you dress attractively and take good care of your body. Physical exercise and regular bathing keep you openly accessible to hugging, snuggling and making love. But true love is more concerned with what's beneath the surface.

Any time you are putting yourself down because you don't think you're attractive enough, you are voting for suffering and against love. No one can win your heart against the powers of your own self-hatred. No one.

Starting today, make the effort to be as physically attractive as you want to be, and then relax into self-acceptance. Know that you can never be loved just for what you look like. Real love is more attracted to what is within.

I am attractive—as is.

❧

I don't stop traffic on a normal day.

Sharon Stone

S mall kindnesses can go a long way to make your life together fun and affectionate. For instance, if you like pears refrigerated and your spouse likes them room temperature, when you return from the market and leave two on the counter and put the rest in the refrigerator— that's a small kindness. No big deal, except you showed your love and respect in a conscious way.

Think of the many small differences you share: You prefer pens/he prefers pencils, you like ginger ale/she likes Perrier, you like reading mystery novels/he gobbles up science fiction, you love classical/she digs jazz. Each of these kinds of differences offers you opportunities to surprise your lover with a small kindness. A pencil with dogs on it left on top of his computer. A small Perrier tucked into her purse. The latest science fiction book left on his pillow. A new jazz CD on the top of her toilet seat.

Small kindnesses—one a day and your heart gets to play!

I can show my love in small ways.

We always wanted to give to each other, no matter how small the giving might have been.

Rolf Lawrence

Everyone suffers from The Fear of Being Beautiful, because we have a hate-love relationship with exceptional success, with great beauty. Tragic really. Because it makes it more difficult to express the God-given bounty that is yours. In Australia they even have a name for the problem: the Tall Poppy Syndrome. You become taller than everyone else and they cut you down.

What if you determine to be the best you can be? What if you will have to leave people behind? Ay, the guilt! Right? Don't fall for it. God is the only force you need answer to, and your own dignity—and they're the same thing.

Love the magnificence that you are. Face the fear of breaking out beyond the limits you inherited. Then do it, with loving passion for the beauty that you are. Do it!

I am beautiful and loving.

❧

You have everything in you that Buddha has,
that Christ has. Your problem is you're afraid to acknowledge
your own beauty. I sit before you and I look and
I see your beauty, even if you don't.

Ram Dass

There are so many prejudices in society about the right way to pair up. The man should make more money than the woman. He should be taller than she is. And the man should be older than the woman, but not by much.

The problem with these prejudices—these prejudgments about other people's lives—is that they are old stereotypes and not relevant to the independence and free choice we enjoy today. Nor are they relevant to the calling of any sincere heart's desire. You see, it's true that love conquers all, if we'll just get our prejudices out of the way.

Let us all reserve judgment about other people's choices. There's no need to feel threatened by or disparaging of the unique pairing of two other people. Perhaps you will discover more about their unique adventure that you can eventually call your own. Keep an open heart about the many ways love can be expressed.

I respect other people's choices.

We don't even consider the sixteen years apart in our age, because we're both basically kids at heart anyway.

Kelly Cline and Bill Sniechowski

If an oyster showed you all that it had endured in order for the pearl to emerge with its magnificent luster and its gracious beauty, you'd probably be shocked. After all, if you want pearls you just go to the store and buy them.

Far too often we expect that, with the price of a wedding license, we can purchase the pearl of eternal love. But just as with the oyster, growing and maturing through the joys and discomforts of real life are necessary—much like what happens to the oyster. In order for you to create a fine enough residence for love to stay, the two of you have to cut and hone your rough edges, which you will inevitably face.

Without the sand in the oyster, you never get the pearl. So, too, with love. If you never have the tensions, if you avoid the conflicts, you can never have the wondrous love that is yours to create.

**I understand that it takes the
sand to get the pearl.**

⁓

The pearl is the oyster's autobiography.

Federico Fellini

Most people hate to fight. But no marriage can remain passionate and fresh if fighting is avoided or abused. Two people living intimately are going to get mad at each other. For sure! But no one gets formal training in Fair Fighting 101. So learn it now.

Fighting Fair in a nutshell: The well-being of your partner is sacred, therefore no dirty fighting; no intention to harm; stick to one issue; express your point of view; avoid blame; listen to each other's position; get to your feelings of hurt, sadness, fear, whatever, as soon as possible because the story isn't the real issue; respect each other's feelings. Find a new way to be with each other that serves you both.

Fighting Fair takes practice. Make sure you both hold your ground. You need to be worthy adversaries so that no one bulldozes the other. Each conflict, fairly fought, will bring you more trust and more tender intimacy.

I will only fight fairly.

❧

I never saw an instance of two disputants
convincing the other by argument.

Thomas Jefferson

D on't be so stubborn. After all, you decided to join your lives together. You can't do that if you both insist on having it only one way and your stubborn ways keep clashing.

You want to be together, right? Well, get creative together when you have to face the challenges and conflicts that come up. Stay conscious of each other's input and support while working out the issues. It will take some time and creativity. But you must stay conscious, otherwise your old stubborn habits will take over and you'll be back in some fight or down in the doldrums, feeling sorry for yourself. Don't let yourself do that.

In order to enjoy each other to the max, you must both stay conscious that you are creating your life together every step of the way. That means choosing to be as loving as possible at all times. That's the conscious creativity of loving every moment, all year long.

**With love and creativity,
we can solve any problem.**

*Creativity can solve almost any problem.
The creative act, the defeat of habit by originality,
overcomes everything.*

George Lois

Do you feel free to share your past with your spouse? If so, wonderful! If not, why not? Why can't you share what you learned about love from your previous partners? Are you struggling with romantic fantasies, wishing you'd been "the one and only"? Or do you still not feel safe and secure with each other?

Love is a skill, a knowing that can only evolve over time—with several partners or with one. To be loved for all that you are while you hide your romantic past is a contradiction in terms. You can't have it both ways.

It's your choice, of course, how well you want to be loved, how much you want to share of yourself. But consider including where you've both come from romantically—all the lessons of love that brought you to where you are today. Wouldn't that be a fuller love, this time around?

> **I recognize that each of my lovers
> taught me to love.**

*With each love relationship,
the soul transforms and the individual's
"partnership with love" evolves.*

Paula Payne Hardin

We bandy about the notion of "the opposite sex" as if men and women are opposite sides of the same coin. But they aren't. They are not opposite anything. They are not, by virtue of their genders, oppositional. They are just different. That's all.

We must change our language to help change our perception of one another. To be "opposite" suggests an underlying animosity and hostility. Then it's a simple step to see romantic relationships as a war between "his way" and "her way"—the "right way" against the "wrong way." And, if opposition is built in, it's but a small and easy step into divorce court. Why? Because the differences are seen as "irreconcilable."

If you truly see things as opposite from each other, and the other's ways are reprehensible or simply nonnegotiable, have the good sense to discover these things early on and please don't marry each other. Otherwise, enjoy your differences. They are not opposites. And neither are the two of you!

I will see my spouse as the "other" sex.

Nothing can vex like the opposite sex.

George Starbuck Galbraith

Hugging, snuggling, holding and cuddling get short shrift in our society. Perhaps because, unlike with sex, you have to surrender emotionally for it to be any fun. There's no goal except the embrace itself, yet you are definitely making love. Feeling one another's warmth, touching each other's skin, perhaps looking into each other's eyes—tenderly surrendered to love.

Do you cuddle when you watch television? Do you hug when you greet each other at the end of the day? Do you snuggle before you fall asleep? Do you ever just hold each other, connecting in the silence and safety of your magical fit? If not, why not?

There are so many opportunities for you to embrace love more fully, by embracing your lover. For the most part, they can fit into activities you already do—like watching television or going to bed together. Time is no excuse. Only the fear of intimacy can hold you back, so curl up, get cozy, relax and let love weave its spell.

I will cuddle and snuggle more.

☙

If you're in each other's arms in silence,
you have it made.

Melody Starr

Whenever you find yourself thinking your spouse (or anyone else) is behaving in a strange way, you can get a better, more loving perspective if you'll remember just one thing. Strange behavior is almost always the by-product of scar tissue around the heart.

Reminding yourself that what's bugging you is probably the manifestation of a scarred heart can be very loving, in and of itself. Otherwise, it's so easy to jump to false conclusions about your lover's motivations. And not only are you wrong, you've provoked a fight by a disrespectful response which, after all, is triggered only by your imaginings.

Let's remember that we all live in a human community with an epidemic of scarred hearts. Compassion can grow and overflow as we learn to understand one another's defenses. At the same time we can soften all our remaining heart space to put a stop to the affliction.

**I will remember that we both have
scar tissue of the heart.**

*So much of the life of mankind,
so many of the events that define human
history are in large part so much
scar tissue over the heart.*

Jacob Needleman

Love is very careful about where it stays. It needs to feel welcome. But welcome on its own terms. As soon as love senses that control, possessiveness or jealousy are surfacing in its name, it takes flight. Love has its pride, after all. It can't afford to be associated with anything but the true nature of itself. When the elusive spirit of love is clung to and grabbed at like a falling sack of flour, love keeps a goodly distance. It is too vulnerable for such rough and rowdy tactics.

For love to feel welcome and want to stay, you must bend your will to the will of love. Not to your idea of it, but to the actual requirements of your love. That is not as difficult as it may sound.

All you need do is remain open. Open and available to the mystery. Then the mystical, mercurial nature of love can wrap itself around you in the silver dawn and you will awaken belonging to one another—freely, openhandedly and with full hearts.

I will hold our love freely.

⤬

Love is like quicksilver in the hand.
Leave the fingers open and it stays.
Clutch it and it darts away.

Dorothy Parker

Why is loving so frightening? And it is! You know it from your own experience. Lots of people are so scared, they prefer chasing the unattainable turn-on, rather than being loved by someone who's right there in front of them.

You see, being loved changes you. And loving changes you. Love is the most powerful change agent on Earth. And it doesn't just stop at some wonderful part of your heart. It goes everywhere inside you. So, when true love is present, all that has never been loved before will come to the surface, because it can and because it must. It can because love makes it feel safe. It must because that's the only way for you to be fully loved.

So have compassion. Loving is a very big deal. It can be scary like a rodeo ride. Just hold on to your hat! The ride will be worth every minute of delicious fear. And then you get past the fear into a kind of lovely bliss . . . and then. . . .

I will continue to push through my fear of love.

❧

The most feared thing in the world is love.
That fear stops most people from being loved and loving.
Together we can release the fear of "I love you."

Albert MacIntyre

Growing up, we're taught to give ourselves over to the more powerful forces of our parents, church and school. We learn to be obedient. We lose ourselves. Then, as adults, we enter into marriage, not having much of a Self. Then we can only lose at love, for no one is at home to navigate the demanding waters of love's course.

For love to grace your life, you must be somebody in your own right. You must continually find and open to your own deep knowings, creative impulses, limitations and strengths. So must your partner. Real love can only grow between two distinctly different Selves.

It is never too late to find your Self. Today, do nothing on automatic pilot. Consciously decide what you will do. Some things you'll have to do even if you don't want to— your family life or work may require it. The point is to be in charge of your Self when you do anything. Practice stating your desires. Practice saying no. Always be in search of your Self.

I'll open up more of my Self today.

❧

But if a man happens to find himself
he has a mansion which he can inhabit with
dignity all the days of his life.

James Michener

Every time your beloved looks into your eyes, he sees a reflection of his value. When your sweetheart gazes upon you, she gets back your vision of her. Your eyes are a window to your soul. But just as certainly, they are a mirror for all who look there.

What do people see of you and of themselves when they look into your eyes? Do you know? Take some time to gaze deeply into your eyes in a mirror when you are alone. What is reflected back? If you feel blessed by what you see, that's wonderful. If you don't like what is mirrored back, then begin to heal whatever is worrying your vision, casting a cloud over your gaze.

Your eyes may not have wanted to see what surrounded you in your youth or in a previous marriage. Their dull expression may be evidence of how they protected you. Now, it's time to see that you are safe and beloved in someone else's eyes.

My eyes are a mirror for my lover.

So the beauty that I saw in everything
the beauty in everything was in her eyes
like the rising of the sun.

Ysaye M. Barnwell

You can never know exactly where love will lead you. You may have a carefully thought-out plan for your life together. Everything may be going exactly as expected. Then, all of a sudden an earthquake destroys your home, a child is struck down with leukemia, one of you is out of work. Now the mystery begins. Now the forces of love invite you to new levels of need and support, fear and freedom, dependence and strength.

When you are responsible to your love, you go where it demands you go—not where you insist you or your partner should go. Your vision will no doubt be more limited than what love will open you to. Love's vision demands that you stay open to the mysterious adventure created by the joining of two lives.

Stay open and aware of the vast mystery of two people coming together to love and be loved through all the amazing and mundane events of your life together. Surrender to the mystery.

I surrender to the unfolding mystery of love.

⨯

*In the deepest sense, to be responsible is
to honor the mystery that lies at the very
heart of every situation.*

Thomas Moore

Many people learned most of what they think about romance in the movies. Did you? It's supposed to be effortless and discomfort-free. Right? It's going to sweep you away to new heights of passion every time you see each other. Sexual ecstasy is guaranteed. And no one ever belches.

But you don't live in the movies. And your love doesn't exist in the movies either. The two of you are part of the real world, with bills to pay and trash to take out. That doesn't mean you can't have an extraordinary love and life. You can. But notice what that means. You just get to be extra-ordinary. Extra-real.

After all, what opens our hearts more than anything is being invited inside someone's very private life. We are touched by their vulnerability. Honored to be trusted so deeply. Excited to know more. Today, invite your lover into a secret part of your heart and make sure to announce how precious this moment is for you. Notice the thrill. Notice how extra-ordinary any moment can be.

I know my life isn't a movie.

*"And they lived happily ever after" is one of
the most tragic sentences in literature.*

Joshua Liebman

Lasting love is an ongoing creation. It's woven together by both people's willingness to be sensitive to each other and be changed by it. The differences between two people often cause difficulty. Some difficulties can't be worked out immediately or even overnight. Requests for change may involve numerous discussions and lots of learning about one another.

Too often people back away from doing this necessary lovework. They give up at the first sign of difficulty or defensiveness. Or they don't even speak up. Don't do that. Don't deprive love of the chance to weave its magical powers as the two of you work out your differences.

Persistence! Persistence! Persistence! It's more powerful than even love. And when the going gets rough, it's even more necessary than the feeling of love. With care and respect, bring up something from which you've backed away. Persist—for as long as it takes and with as many breaks as may occur—until you are both satisfied and enhanced by the outcome.

My persistence pays off.

❦

*Nothing in the world can take
the place of persistence.*

Calvin Coolidge

What's the big deal about apologizing? So many of us have such a hard time getting the words "I'm sorry" out of our mouths, much less with sincere, loving feeling. Is it that we'll lose pride, or tenderize some of the toughness around our heart? What do you lose? What makes it so hard to say "I'm sorry"?

If you can't feel genuinely sorry when you've hurt your spouse, then you're not really involved emotionally in your marriage. Something else has your commitment—like an image of yourself as perfect or impenetrable. Aw, shucks, give it up! Open your heart to the pain of your honey. Get over the pride and apologize. Mean it from the bottom of your heart. And make a commitment to change whatever you did.

You're not bad. You're human. Humans make mistakes. Humans can be shortsighted and hurt their loved ones. That's life. But that doesn't excuse not apologizing for doing it. Go ahead: Apologize right now!

I apologize with love when I've hurt my spouse.

*When you say "I'm sorry," look the
person in the eye.*

Tantra Totem

Are you a collector? Do you already have a collection that represents your marriage in some way? If not, consider the fun and sentiment of collecting something together that involves how you feel for each other, or something you both love.

For instance, if you decorate for the winter holidays, you might want to incorporate an ongoing collection of photos of the two of you together in holiday frames. If you both love a particular animal, you might collect them—as statues, figurines or the print on your sheets. If you travel, you might collect mementos from all your favorite places. The point is not to collect dust catchers, but to enjoy and display your love in a special way.

If you decide to start a love collection, be sure it's something you both want to do. Do not strap your budget, and avoid becoming obsessed. The point is to love doing it together.

**I can help us create a special collection
that expresses our love.**

❧

The real key to collecting is just have fun.

Janet Bodnar

There's not a married person alive who hasn't wondered what it would be like with someone else. The grass can look mighty green over there, where you have no real experience, just the fantasies you concoct.

But you were attracted to your spouse for very good reasons. Even if you're having trouble, you can work together to solve it and end up even tighter and more intimate than before. Of course, over on that greener grass you think you'd just be able to nap all day and make love all night. Not true. Think about all the people you've met who seemed so pulled together at first—you know, their lawn was sooooo green— and then, to mix a metaphor, you realized they were rowing with just one oar—not so green after all.

You can help yourself avoid the grass-is-greener syndrome. Stay clear about the real blessings of your spouse and your relationship. Besides, to keep it sooooo green you'd have to run behind pushing the fertilizing machine every day. Take a break. Have a glass of iced tea and enjoy the lawn.

**I know the greener grass is only
greener on the surface.**

~

*Why should I go out for a hamburger
when I have steak at home?*

Paul Newman

August

Earth's crammed with heaven,
And every common bush afire with God;
But only he who sees takes off his shoes;
The rest sit round it and pluck blackberries.

ELIZABETH BARRETT BROWNING

L ove and pleasure are often forbidden. Yet their promise shouts out from billboards, movies and novels. Do you say, "No, no, that's not allowed, not for me. I need to be good"? If so, you're far from alone. Many marriages are saddled with the shame-filled residue of strict upbringing and fear of surrendering to pleasure.

We aren't referring to anything immoral, only pleasures that loosen up your desires, your vulnerabilities, your ability to love. Pleasures may be sexual, but may just as well be out-of-control laughter or dishes left in the sink to get to dance class. Anything fun that invites you to be more of who you really are.

Pleasure can have an edge of naughtiness. Is that okay with you? Or does it make you feel guilty? As long as it's not against your morality, if pleasure touches into shame or guilt, now's the time to heal those old wounds and let them go, so you can have more fun and more love in your life.

I enjoy pleasure without guilt.

The best pleasures of this world are not quite pure.

Goethe

Do you have a camera that's gathering dust? Or do you use it to document your kids' lives but forget that your marriage is growing and changing, too? Maybe you have lots of photos but they're all in the attic.

As a gift to your life together, get creative and develop some kind of ongoing Love Book or Love Collage with lots and lots of photographs of just the two of you. (You can do the same with your family photos, but keep this special just for the two of you—an example of real romance for your kids to see.) You might want to add other mementos and write in funny comments.

Keep lots of film on hand. Document anything that's meaningful to the two of you. Ask waiters, other tourists, anyone handy to take your photo. Enjoy the intimacy of being romantic for the camera. Then, every so often, take a lovers' stroll down memory lane and admire the life you keep creating together.

I will take more photographs of us together.

❧

*Documenting our life together, having
a photographic record of our relationship,
is a blessing to our love.*

Elizabeth Asunsolo

236

All around you is the miracle of nature. God's precious gift of every variety of tree, flower, cloud and bird. Raindrops and snowflakes are never like one another. A spectacle of magnificence. Free to you from God.

How often do you take time to open your heart to nature's blessings? Or do you just take for granted the life around you? If so, that keeps your heart closed and your soul unfed. One of the simplest ways to learn more about love is to experience the awe that nature can call forth. The magic of a rainbow. A bird's morning trill. Butterflies, night-blooming jasmine, even those roly-poly bugs or a moth at a flame.

Every day, feast your eyes and heart on the other forms of life that share the planet with you. Allow for amazement, wonder and love for the Creator who did all this. And know that this, too, is love.

Nature opens my heart to love.

⁂

I remember once seeing the early morning light
of dawn and being filled with love for
the awesome possibility of life.

Denny LeClear

B eing "in love" is really make-believe. When you love someone, you love them for who they are. When you're in love, anything from lust to laughter can prompt you to call it *love,* because when you're in love, you become a servant to the feeling, rather than a participant in a relationship.

In the beginning you can be in love all you want, but if you do not graduate to loving the other person, you stay in emotional adolescence. And it's in the name of being "in love" that so many childish and even dangerous sins of love get acted out—spying on him when he's out with the boys, looking through her wallet, listening to his answering machine, checking out her e-mail. And even worse: jealous fits, control of her time and whereabouts, hitting each other, revenge against his late nights at work. All in the name of being in love.

Don't give your heart to being "in love." Love the one you're with.

My goal is love, not being in love.

The difference between loving someone
and being in love is akin to kneeling on the ground
versus being a midget.

Joel Achenbach

L oving well is not just an affair of the heart. It's also the product of a mind well used.

If you only trust your feelings, you can lose out on love. Not because your heart's out to lunch, but because it may get so swept up in hope and lust that it ignores that your "lover" is not really a candidate for intimacy. Or, if you've been terribly hurt by what you called "love," your heart may be so shut down it won't budge even for the greatest person on Earth.

So, stay alert. Don't let yourself get manipulated. Think things through. If things are moving too fast and you don't feel just right, stop and think about what's going on. What is happening that makes you feel anxious or scared? No doubt, you'll be able to think it through and clear your head so you can respond in a solid, mature manner.

Respect that God gave you both a brain and a heart. Never sacrifice one for the other

I will use my head, not just my heart.

People always say, "Let your heart tell you what to do."
Well, your heart sometimes is bruised and it
doesn't serve you well to be emotional.

Kevin Costner

D o you enjoy when strangers smile at you? Or do you feel suspicious? Do you smile back? If not, why not? Unless you could be in physical danger by appearing to invite further contact, what do you have to lose in smiling at others? Nothing but your habitual distance from connecting with those around you.

Smile. That's right, take this moment and smile. Once you're smiling, try to feel depressed. Pretty difficult, right? When you smile you give your body and your soul a positive, feel-good message. When you smile at others, you give them a little taste of love.

As part of your daily meditation on practical spirituality, be sure to include smiling at others. Smile more at your spouse. See what happens. Smile more at your children. See what happens. Smile at the people you work with, especially those you really like. See what happens. Notice how a simple smile can transform the moment. Notice how you feel even more loving.

I smile lovingly at the world.

Smiling is mouth yoga.

Thich Nhat Hanh

N o one ever has a feeling, an emotion, out of nowhere. It always arises from the person's life experience, which colors the current moment, triggering a specific meaning and response. That's why two people often have different responses to the same situation.

Rather than arguing about your differing reactions, ask your spouse why she feels the way she does, ask him what triggered his feelings. Know that your feelings are meaningful, too, and you'll get the chance to express them. But for now, listen with care. You are at the heart of the heart of love. It is a time of tender intimacy when your private realities arc shared—when you go beneath the surface to meet each other in a new way.

Whenever you don't immediately understand your spouse's response, ask for more information. Go beyond the obvious. You'll love each other more deeply for the distinctly unique individuals that you are.

I commit to finding out what's behind the feelings.

The moment we find the reason behind the emotion ...
the wall we have built is breached. That's why it pays to ask those
painful questions. The answers can set you free.

Gloria Steinem

In fairy tales, the prince and princess have to overcome many obstacles before they can live "happily ever after." But they never have to learn about receiving love, conflict resolution or developing a budget. They never have to grasp the spiritual significance of their differences. They already know it all.

But we humans are not born knowing how to love, much less how to create a lifelong, passionate marriage. In fact, the love we see lighting the eyes of a baby is its delight in your attention. We have to outgrow this self-centered way of connecting and learn the thinking and feeling skills that allow us to love one another with value and respect for the differences.

The early days of marriage can be tough, when fairy-tale expectations are strong and emotional skills are weak. Many couples get stuck there and fail. But love requires us to do the lovework of sharpening our heart skills. And marriage is the best classroom!

I commit to learning the skills of love.

The expectations of life depend upon diligence;
the mechanic that would perfect his work
must first sharpen his tools.

Confucius

Ever notice that your fights always end up feeling much the same? Oh, the topic, the behavior that started it may vary. But over and over, you seem to get right back to some kind of core problem with each other. That's exactly what happens. That's why fighting can't be resolved well if you just change surface behaviors to "fix" it.

You see, all fights are about hurt feelings. The hurt can take many forms—feeling disappointed, betrayed, abandoned, ignored, put down, insulted . . . on and on. Each of you brought old emotional wounds into your marriage. When you get hurt, it touches these old wounds and the pain is fierce. That's where the fight has to be resolved: in respecting and healing emotional injuries by becoming more sensitive to them.

Always fight fair. Be sympathetic to each other's hurt. Remember you love each other. Open to help heal one another through love. Remember you are allies.

I will help us get to the real issue of our fights.

The fights in most relationships add up to about one fight.
One fight, with infinite ways of showing itself.

Cheryl Meiser

How is it that we're kind to strangers who seek directions, strange dogs and even the strange neighbor asking to borrow something, yet we often fail to be kind to our spouse? Some say "familiarity breeds contempt," but if that's the case it's breeding that's at fault, not familiarity. Why? Because familiarity very often breeds love and respect.

When you were a kid, how did your parents treat each other? Was it with care and tender respect? Or was it with dismissal, bad jokes and even emotional and/or physical abuse? If you're in the first group, it probably takes very little consciousness for you to be kind to your spouse. Why? Because that's what you saw. If you're in the second group, it will require a great deal more consciousness to make sure you are kind to your spouse.

Either way, the discipline of kindness is necessary, especially when you're mad or hurt. And for the sake of your love and your own self-respect, be kind!

I commit to being consciously kind.

❦

*I truly believe in the "discipline of kindness,"
meaning not just when it's convenient for me, but to
always have kindness in my consciousness.*

Devers Branden

We are a society of addicts. Whether it's food, alcohol, legal and illegal drugs, sex, gambling, gossip, romance novels or whatever it may be—people need their "fix." The question is: What is everyone trying to fix?

With your addiction to television, the Internet, working out, the rat race, going to the doctor, etc., what are you trying to fix? Avoiding pain? Comforting yourself? Trying to make up for insecurity? What if, at some time earlier in your life, you tasted ecstasy and you're unconsciously trying to get it back by hanging on to substitutes, not knowing how to find the real thing?

Substitutes never work. They just intensify the addiction, the need to fix something.

The ecstasy you've been seeking is real. It's right there in every breath, every breeze, every blessing. Soar!

I relinquish substitutes.

❧

The craving for ecstasy has led to the most characteristic symptom of our time: addictive behavior.

Robert Johnson

People use the word "tolerate" as if that's the best we can do when it comes to respect for diversity. For example, parents will say, "You know how your mother is" or "Your dad's just like that, humor him." That's tolerance. Is that what you want from your spouse? Your kids? The people at work? Hardly!

Certainly there are people who can be very, very difficult. You may have in-laws or neighbors who are extremely pushy or intrusive, unkind or abusive. But don't tolerate them. Stop them from mistreating you. If you're worried about hurting their feelings—please, in the name of love, put your feelings first. It is never, never loving to allow someone to mistreat you!

If you feel that your spouse is tolerating you, your attitudes or behaviors—please insist on discussing the problem. Express your hurt feelings. Explore the issues fully, so that you can develop respect between you, not tolerance. Value your differences, don't tolerate them. Tolerance is prejudice with a smile.

I look beyond tolerance to find value.

I don't want anyone to just tolerate me!

Ann Matvchuk

Whether it's gliding around the floor cheek-to-cheek or putting the groove on the moves, dancing is the closest thing to physically making love. You feel each other's body, touch each other's skin, get in synch with the rhythm, move together, breathe, look into one another's eyes. You're hot and moist. Close, surrendered to the moment. You're together on the dance floor, opening to the enjoyment of your relationship. Ahhhhhhh . . .

If you aren't already comfortable dancing, perhaps it would be fun to take dance lessons. It might be ballroom dancing, swing, jazz, square dancing, line dancing, you name it. Whatever would be fun for the two of you together.

Make dates to dance. You might even clear the furniture, turn on your favorite music and dance in your living room. Express your love through your body, surrender to the passion that wants to express itself in dance. Admire each other's courage and form. Love it—you're movin' to the groovin'!

I feel sexy and romantic when we're dancing.

❧

*Dancing is a perpendicular expression
of a horizontal desire.*

Source Unknown

You've no doubt heard that love means to sacrifice, to put someone else's good ahead of your own. This notion has been part of Western civilization for twenty-five hundred years. But, does this idea of love insist you come in second? If so, that kind of "love" can only lead to resentment and a sense of being cheated.

Nevertheless, the Bible is clear: Love thy neighbor as thyself. Not more. Not differently. The same as. So, the challenge is to know and love your Self so that you can genuinely love others.

Do you consider your opinions, desires and idiosyncrasies as much as you do your lover's? In the name of self-love, do you know what you need from your relationship? It's essential that you listen with respect and value to your Self. If you don't, you will never be able to truly hear your partner, your neighbor or anyone else. Remember, not more, not differently—but as.

I am as important to me as my lover is to me.

※

Thou shalt love thy neighbor as thyself.

Jesus Christ

It's not always easy to be enthusiastic about your relationship. When the bills have strained your budget, the kids are sick, or you have a toothache, enthusiasm has to take a back seat to steady determination and taking care of yourself. But when you can call up your excitement, your passion for living a life of discovery with the one you love, what could be better?

Whenever a stream of enthusiasm accompanies your day, the slightest effort can be filled with a generosity of spirit. The most difficult task can be permeated with the fire of love, fueling your energy, outwitting your self-doubt. Tap into your enthusiasm when you and your spouse are sharing a private moment and watch the glow of your shared love expand and fill the two of you.

Commit yourself to sharing your enthusiasm, allowing it to be communicable throughout your family. And don't forget to celebrate your spouse's enthusiasm as well!

I embrace the journey of love with enthusiasm.

Enthusiasm—inspired or possessed
by the God within.

Webster's Unabridged Dictionary

Are the two of you competitive—with each other? What if you took that impulse and competed over which of you loves the other more? Will your spouse play? If not, rethink your relationship: Do you really have one? Or, do you look forward to having a great time playing the daily championship love game.

Remember this is the Love Game. It's not about winning. It's about loving! The point is to have a good time creatively competing to express your love for each other. It's about turning your competitive impulse into an ever-excellent, ever-deepening love and intimacy.

You could even have prizes. At the end of the day, you could agree on the winner who could choose: a) a shoulder rub; b) a foot rub; c) whatever—you name it!

I will show I love more.

❧

Spend each day trying to prove which one
of you loves the other more.

Sharon Smiley Lusk and Brad Lusk

When you consistently say or think, "Whatever you want, Dear," that's a clear sign that you're not alive inside your relationship. You're there to please, satisfy and service the needs of your partner. What you need doesn't matter. You may be so practiced at ignoring yourself, you no longer know what you need. And you call this "love." It's not.

If you're in jeopardy of losing yourself in the name of love, you must learn to love your own needs and desires. Only then can you sincerely begin to know true love. Don't be passive about what you want. Speak up about what movie you'd like to see, what kind of food you want for dinner. Have an opinion about where to go on your Sunday drive or next year's vacation—anything!

It takes two to make love—in and out of bed. Show up. Be somebody. Your love needs you to be you!

I will not lose myself to love.

Sometimes in a relationship, you start to
think so much about the other person that you
kind of end up losing sight of yourself.

Christian Slater

Take a minute to visualize how you want your relationship to be five years from now. Imagine both of you at your most magnificent and your most loving. Now add to your visualization the lifestyle you want in five years. Feel, in your body, how it would be to actually live the life you can see in your mind's eye.

Congratulations! You've just taken the first step to letting visualization help you develop the life you truly want. The power is in using the process every day, believing it's yours to have and guiding your daily behavior to support it. The process is even more powerful if the two of you are joined in desiring the same thing and you visualize it together.

As often as you want, call up your visualization and feel in your body the passion you have for it. Commit to it with your whole being. Go for it! Be it!

**I can help create my romantic future
by visualizing it.**

⁂

*I visualized where I wanted to be,
what kind of player I wanted to become.
I knew exactly where I wanted to go, and
I focused on getting there.*

Michael Jordan

Some people treat food like a short-order cook in a cheap diner. Slap it together. Throw it on a plate. Drop it on the table. What could be more unappealing and unappetizing?

Food is a central part of our lives. Why not put your love and care into creating wonderful meals? Why not sit down to meals served with flair and individuality? Of course there are times you just want to order in pizza. But you can still have lovely napkins and fun beverage glasses.

When you put love into food, you begin to open your attention to the world of mealtimes. You can have fun by playing with how you display food or by inventing playday meals when you serve breakfast at dinner time and dessert before the main course or whatever the playday spirit moves you to do. Feed each other with your fingers as part of foreplay. Make love to your spouse, starting (or ending) with a favorite sensuous meal. *Bon appétit!*

I will put a lot of love into our food and mealtimes.

A big pot of vegetable soup, simmering on the stove, nourishes the heart of a home. Especially on a cold day, it speaks and tastes and smells like love.

Corinne Edwards

It can seem that we are so small, merely a speck in the totality of life. And at the physical level, of course, that's true. But there is much more to our existence with one another, and with all of life, than meets the eye.

When we look beyond the physical, we enter the larger domain of spirit, where energy transcends matter. Where the energy of love takes us into regions of faith, our love can reach out soul to soul, healing the distance we ordinarily accept. For it is at the level of soul that we celebrate our differences, knowing they are the creative way each of us physically expresses spirit.

Can you see that our individual differences are God's invitation to truly love all of creation? And when we do, the miracle that is our beloved is no longer merely a speck, but a reflection of all love.

My spirit soars when I give myself over to love.

❧

Love goes very far beyond the physical person and the beloved. It finds its deepest meaning in his spiritual being, his inner self.

Viktor Frankl

It's just so easy to see your spouse's behavior as "wrong," "stupid" or "silly." Why? Because we were all raised to view one another's differences with suspicion and negative judgment. It's almost natural to write someone off because of the way they wear their hair, landscape their lawn or speak out (or not) at a meeting. We act like the other person is a virus or bacteria waiting to infect us, and our immune system must attack to keep us healthy.

Now, we must make judgments; otherwise we cannot be decisive or discerning. But that's no excuse for treating your spouse and others in ways that banish or punish them simply because you don't like their ways. That's just a form of violence.

You can contribute to reducing the violence—caused by the threat and hatred of differences—by changing your vision to make differences interesting and curious, rather than condemnable. That way you are a force for respect and love, rather than hate and violence.

I will avoid making negative judgments.

Judgment is the mud you sling at your
own happiness and well-being.

Source Unknown

There's more to you than meets the eye. True enough. There's also more to you than you know. When true love is present, it will have its ways with you—beckoning you, prodding you, safely guiding you to discover more of you than you'd ever imagined existed.

Your spouse may have glimpsed the depth of your character, or a special joy that had yet to catch flame when the two of you first met. Maybe you were never allowed to be a kid when you were little, and all it takes is your spouse's enjoyment for the kid to come out to play. Sometimes it just takes that special chemistry to release some of your secret treasures.

Open to your lover's desire to know you more fully. Open to the magic of loving discovery. When you do, you give permission for love to mine the deeper aspects of your being, to support you in moving from caterpillar to glorious butterfly.

I allow my lover to open me to myself.

◈

I found someone ... who was there for me
and brought out things in me that
I didn't know I had.

Liam Neeson

Romance, hearts and flowers, passionate lovemaking, fun, freedom—that's the image on wedding day! Then, after the honeymoon, along come the bills, the dirty dishes, the hair in the bathroom sink, the trash. And that's all part of marriage, too. But so many people aren't ready for the responsibility of those everyday chores, the routine upkeep of a home.

Real love and successful marriage is for grown-ups. You can't just play at love. Yet, so many people trash their marriage rather than happily taking out the trash.

With an openhearted vision of your marriage, everything you do to support your life together becomes part of loving. You may need to negotiate who does what and when and how and even how often, but you avoid butting heads in competition over who's the most victimized, who does "most of the chores." You gladly do what's needed, knowing your spouse is doing the same. Maybe they're not even "chores" anymore, but just acts of love!

As an expression of love, I do my share of the chores.

Marriage is not just spiritual communion and passionate embraces; marriage is also three meals a day and remembering to carry out the trash.

Joyce Brothers

Sex, sex, sex. It's so hot and urgent in the beginning. Then after awhile it becomes routine at best, nonexistent in many cases. That's when so many couples get into trouble. They assume that because their sexual heat has burned out, that means love has too. But this doesn't have to be the case.

The problem is that all of our public images of sex are of the conquest-and-seduction variety, the stuff that happens at the beginning. We see almost nothing that represents the mature, sacred sexuality that can only occur in long-term marriages, when trust is high and love is deep. Only then can we truly make love with our bodies, for only then is commitment in place and we feel safe enough to open our soul as well as our body.

Make a date to explore your sexuality as true lovemaking. Use your body as a medium of passionate creativity. Let your body express your love. Enjoy the heat and the heart, the sweet and sweat. Give your body permission to express your emotional as well as physical pleasure. Be fully present in your body.

Sex can be sacred when I love with my body.

Sex is an emotion in motion.
Love is what you make it and who you make it with.

Mae West

Deep below the crust of your spouse's social façade, there lives a magnificent soul, a being whose truth is undeniably beautiful. Don't go looking at surface appearance, though it may be quite appealing. Don't go poking around in ambition or success, though it may be very impressive. But to grasp the awesome beauty of your partner, open yourself to the wonders of his tenderness and care for you, her commitment to helping your community, his weeping for life's tragedies, her open abandon when making love.

Look there, in the beauty of the unglamorous but humbling magnificence of truth.

You may be tempted to draw back from the intensity, the embarrassing rawness. For the truth may seem too much. It may knock at your own heart to open toward the spiritual center of your truth. Do not turn away. Love is calling you forward into the deepest part of your Self.

Today, stay open to be touched, as deeply as possible, by the beauty that is at the heart of the person you love.

I see the beauty in your truth.

Get to know the truthful, if you would
become acquainted with beauty.

Paul Williams

Domestic violence is usually described as solely physical and male-initiated. Women are innocent victims. But let's get real here. Domestic violence is anything aimed at hurting the other person. Vicious words can hurt very deeply. And women are fully capable of initiating physical violence against men, and they do.

Any time you dish out verbal or physical violence—or you put up with being on the receiving end—you violate yourself and the love you claim to feel. You also teach your children that it is okay to abuse people in the name of love. You may have been raised in an abusive household. You may not even know what's over the line, because you've not yet realized that your parent(s) were way out of line with you. Here's the guideline: Anything intended to hurt another person is violence and it's abuse.

Stay conscious of any impulse to wound your spouse or your child, or to take it on the chin yourself. Don't do it! Just don't do it!

I commit to no verbal or physical hitting.

Richard Gelles and Murray Straus find high levels of violence in many American families, but in both of their national surveys they found that women were just as likely to engage in it as men.

Christina Hoff Sommers

L ife can be a very lonely walk, whether married or alone, if you don't have an intimate, loving relationship, at least with a friend. Intimacy is the experience of being emotionally or physically vulnerable, revealing your Self and being consciously and actively received—seen, heard and understood—by another. Real love can only occur when two people do this with and for each other—and often.

We are not taught how to receive one another so fully, so completely. As humans we do not automatically have the desire or the skill to open our hearts with full desire to know one another, yet we all desire to be known in just that way. We must learn to do this in our romantic relationships if they are ever to thrive and nourish our souls.

In some way, ask your special love to know you more fully today. Then, open your curiosity to know your partner in a deeply personal way as well. Be respectful of any anxiety or fear that you may experience. No matter how well you know each other, intimacy asks that you be learners.

I'm aware that intimacy takes both of us.

*Love from one being to another can only
be that two solitudes come nearer, recognize and
protect and comfort each other.*

Han Suyin

Maria Shriver is a dyed-in-the-wool Democrat. Arnold Schwarzenegger is a true-blue Republican. And they're married to each other. Melissa is a UCLA alum who roots for the Bruins. Andy graduated from USC and cheers for the Trojans. They are crosstown rivals and married to each other.

Clearly there are some things that are very important that you don't want to change. And unless your position affects the health or safety of you, your spouse or your kids, why would you need to? On these kinds of issues—whether it's politics or how you like your meat cooked—what do you lose if you agree to disagree? Only your righteousness and control.

What do you gain? You get to sincerely love someone who is not just like you. You learn that you can share a life that has fundamental differences as a basis for respect and value and even excitement. You expand your mind and your heart. And your soul dances with glee when you agree to disagree!

I can agree to disagree and respect our differences.

*We never compromised. We negotiated, and what we
could not negotiate we agreed to disagree on.*

Richard Hoyt

I t's so easy to find fault, even in the name of love. We've all done it. Pick, pick, pick. Complain, complain, complain. The result: impotence, hopelessness, failure.

But if it were love that guided your attention, wouldn't it be more caring to focus on bringing out the very best in your spouse? Supporting new freedom, greater confidence and a larger life? Oh sure, there's always room for specific changes, because each of us could learn a thing or two that would make us healthier, more gracious or more socially appropriate. But it does no good to continually complain and critique.

Think about your lover's strong points and undeveloped gifts. How can you support her in trying new things that would build her confidence? What can you say about his talents that would support his growth? Remember, your lover wants to excel, and it's your love and support that can provide the kind of spiritual cheerleading needed to spur the leap.

I focus on bringing out the best in my spouse.

The challenge for men and women in the twenty-first century is not to find what's wrong with each other but to continually ask, "How can we bring out the BEST in each other?"

Robert C. Ware

There are plenty of crises that invite you to go the extra mile in expressing your love. Don't confuse this with martyrdom. If you do, it'll kill you.

When you're called upon to go out of your way, do you moan and sulk or do you enjoy helping the one you love? If you protest, you need to change your vision from self-centered to more openhearted. Get some practice. For instance, start dinner and turn on the Jacuzzi for her when she gets home. Wash his car while he's napping. Design a piece of jewelry for her anniversary present and have it made. Take the kids out while he's pushing to meet a weekend deadline and return with his favorite sandwich and beer. Not huge stuff, but they require that you stretch.

Then when the next crisis occurs you'll be ready to, well, install a new toilet at 10 P.M. the night before a party you're giving the next day—and you'll do it with love.

I will go the extra mile.

❧

Love means going the extra mile with a smile.

Barbara Steffin and Nick Rath

Do you recycle? Do the two of you spread your love out to the Earth, to other forms of life, by making an effort to preserve our natural resources? If not, one way to expand your capacity to love, and have fun together, is to become more conscious about and get involved with ecological activities.

You can begin with recycling: Save your aluminum cans, bottles and jars, plastic containers, newspaper and mail/office paper. Find out how your recycling drop-off wants them organized. Then, every so often, go together and deliver your love-gifts to the Earth. You may get money for some of it. If so, throw it in a jug, save it up and send it off to your favorite "green" organization. Be gentle with the Earth. Turn off unnecessary lights. Start a compost heap. Plant trees.

Get involved with anything that's fun and helps the Earth to support your life. When you love all of life, and see how all of life is interdependent, that's ecological consciousness.

I lovingly protect the well-being of the planet.

Revolutionary consciousness is to be found
Among the most ruthlessly exploited masses:
Animals, trees, water, air, grasses.

Gary Snyder

September

*One does not "fall into"
commitments. They are purposeful,
intentional decisions of a mature and
disciplined person who engages himself or
herself to act in a certain way over
a given period of time.*

VICTOR L. BROWN JR.

In the old intimacy, the man did "the man thing" and the woman did "the woman thing" and neither "the twain shall meet" except in bed and at the dinner table. One of them, usually the man, took the dominant role in decision making and the other, usually the woman, followed. Fortunately all that stereotyping is going the way of other prejudicial categories, leaving us free to know each other for our unique individuality.

In the new intimacy, marriage is a team thing. Both people participate in decision making and both offer their expertise and talent to the financial ledger and the home and family caretaking. Intimacy is no longer primarily sexual, since both people get to be respected and valued for the very different individuals that they are. And the team is engaged in fulfilling joint and individual goals, a kind of daily meditation on practical spirituality.

Assess how well you're doing as a team player, and that means insisting your partner is one as well.

I relish being a team player.

In a relationship you have to meet in the middle.
It's not coach and player. It's a team.

Julia Roberts

It may be difficult to understand how your spouse can be totally committed to you and to a very demanding, ambitious career, or vice versa. Many people wreck their relationships by competing with their lover's beloved career, and consequently end up losing.

Because love and work are the two major areas we have for self-expression, balancing the two can sometimes be very difficult. Fairly often a spouse's corporate demands or the requirements of a privately held business can clash with the emotional desires and family schedule of a homemaker or a spouse who works nine to five. As long as you recognize you can never be the only focus of your spouse's passions, you will save yourself from foolish competition.

Both of you must remember that you're creating your life together. No one can be self-centeredly ignoring the needs and complaints of the other. Just as well, compassion and sensitivity are necessary to get through the challenging times, with love as your central focus.

I will not compete with my spouse's career.

Music is my mistress, and she plays
second fiddle to no one.

Duke Ellington

E very so often, one or both of you feel the urge to change the way you're living. It may hit one or both of you. There's a kind of urgency or even profound boredom announcing that it's time to reconstruct your life together. It's just a time of upheaval and renewal. Simply put, you've outgrown the lifestyle you've been living.

Many people misunderstand these feelings of boredom and agitation as a sign their relationship is over. So they break up or divorce. But that's a choice driven by ignorance. When we understand that love will always move us to expand and better ourselves, we can know in advance that the urge to renew our relationship will occur every so often.

Allow love to move you beyond your imagination, beyond what is already known. Let the energies of love open your life, give rise to new goals and renew you in ways never before felt.

I can renew love by renewing myself.

Sometimes a life, like a house, needs renovating,
the smell of new wood, new rooms in the heart, unimagined
until one begins the work. One rebuilds because
the structure deserves a renewing.

Doris Schwerin

U sed to be that if you carried the same name and the same bloodline, that was enough to make you family. That was when kinship and survival were closely tied together. But now we can have so much more, and we want it.

We want a family that understands and supports us. We want to explore our spirituality and advance in the world. And to have this growth-inspiring family, we have to create it—every day. We have to juggle schedules, communicate with respect for conflicting needs, and maybe even negotiate where in the world to live. Family is a daily, active, loving verb.

To help create a loving family, hold family meetings, even if it's just the two of you. Make an agenda of issues that impact on being the kind of family each of you wants. Discuss solutions with loving respect for all points of view. Be patient. Some issues will take time to resolve. Be a family of conscious love.

I actively create a loving family.

※

You do family—it's a verb, not a noun.

Charles Darrah

Any time a couple brags they never fight, they've either defined fighting as too dangerous or one or both of them is emotionally dead. A healthy fight, out of love for each other, is an expression of respect for the needs of the relationship to change. Healthy fighting addresses an issue that's required for the vitality of the relationship. This kind of fight is a catalyst for growth and new intimacy.

When you avoid fighting, you cheat on your relationship. You hide your real feelings and put forward a fake front. Both of you know something's wrong, but it can't be acknowledged. A healthy fight gets stuff out in the open, stuff that may be pretty hard to take when it finally surfaces—but now you can both deal with it and grow your relationship in a new, healthier direction.

Don't cheat on your relationship today. Express your anger, be willing to fight for your love.

**I will fight for love, rather than
cheat on my relationship.**

*The only failure I know is never
making the attempt.*

George Clooney

Most people remember to celebrate birthdays, anniversaries and holidays. What about your personal triumphs—a promotion at work, your first garden, winning an award, completing a class, a new car, passing a test and . . . you name it? These are exciting times. One or both of you jumped over a hurdle and won! Celebrate! Celebrate success as a special time of joyous intimacy.

You may want to be spontaneous and ride the whim for each notable event. Or you might want to develop a family ritual for particular kinds of celebrations—something everyone really enjoys together. It could be your favorite champagne with a special meal, a trip to a special place, a particular dessert, whatever expresses your joy and pleasure in one another's success.

And don't forget to celebrate one another for even smaller things—a different haircut, the installation of a new computer, saying "No" when it's been difficult—all fun reasons for receiving hugs and kisses! Embrace any reason to celebrate yourselves!

I make it a point to celebrate our life.

A celebration can be a ritual, a time of sharing together,
or a moment of giving thanks—a refresher, a reminder of
all that we are and all that we have together.

Gale and Michael Cohen

When you're married, you want many things to be different than they are. Lots of folks end up in divorce court because they insist these changes occur NOW. But that's the result of misunderstanding the ways of change.

As adults we still learn very much like toddlers: We need to look at stuff from various angles, shake it a bit, leave it alone for awhile and then come back and master it. That's like the learning curve in a relationship—though some things can take a while to master. So, with your spouse you can't insist on one-stop learning. You must ask for what you want, perhaps offer loving reminders from time to time and have patience to know that what you want, if it's realistic, will occur.

With infinite patience, you surrender the time frame for getting what you want. You have complete faith that it will occur and you relax and live in peace and love. Why wouldn't your spouse want to change in such a loving, respectful environment?

I surrender my desires to infinite patience.

Infinite patience produces immediate results.

A Course in Miracles

R un here. Go there. Work. Plan a party. Play with kids. Entertain relatives. Business meeting. School Open House. Someone's birthday. Cook dinner. Take out trash. Go to sleep. Sound anything like your life? Yes, you're no doubt very busy. But what's missing in this list of stuff? More important than anything else? Enjoy your spouse!

Whether you're shopping together, cleaning the house together, or at the boss's dinner party together, enjoy your spouse! You are love companions, not just roommates. Every activity you do together can be significantly more fun when you play with each other, flirt, give each other that special look, get one another's opinion, chat about what's going on, stay emotionally connected. Why be married and then just go through the motions of your day together?

Keep your partner in your awareness. Remember what it was like when you were single. Notice the gratitude you feel for having such a good friend, a fun playmate and lover. Enjoy your spouse!

I consciously enjoy my lover.

❧

Aboard a ferry, I asked what he thought was the best part of the trip. Without a moment's hesitation, he replied, "You." Could there ever be a response as romantic as that?

Sandy Jasmer

D o you feel that no one listens to you? Frustrated, you raise your voice, or repeat everything over and over. In the name of loving self-respect, it's time for you to give that up.

Nagging is a symptom of poor communication skills. It either means you don't state your original message or request in a firm, confident, grown-up manner, or that you deliver the information when your spouse isn't available to really hear you—watching TV, getting ready for work, taking care of the kids. Either way, you probably suffer from an unconscious attachment to not being taken seriously, to not being heard.

It's time for you to grow past this underhanded way of frustrating yourself and your partner. From now on, when you have an important message, start by asking for her attention, make eye contact with him, and deliver your information in a respectful, clear and direct manner. Check to make sure your lover understood you. Nagging is a drag!

I speak clearly and don't have to repeat myself.

❦

Once said is information.
Twice said is nagging.

Corinne Balzac

Even if you don't have children, and increasingly couples are choosing not to, the kids around you need your love. They need to feel you notice them as unique, one of a kind. They need your respect for their creativity, ingenuity, humor, athletic ability—whatever you can consciously notice and admire.

How we love our children, so goes the world! Only if they feel respected do they learn respect for all life. Only if kids are loved for their differences can they learn to receive love. Express your love through respect and value for the individuality of each child.

Honor the children in your life. Give them your delight for the magic of their differences. That's the love each child so dearly needs!

I will teach love to the children.

*Hug your kids and tell them you love them
as much as you can and mean it.*

Liam Neeson

We're all so protective of our hearts. We play it "close to the vest" so that our hearts won't be broken. Yet, isn't it true that we wait, aching to be known by at least one, just one, special person, the person who loves us well enough to break open our heart?

Please risk yourself with the one you love. Let your heart break open. Let the flood of life pour out in rushing tensions of joy and rage, laughter and hurt—and be met by love.

It's really true that when we're allowed deep into anyone's heart, we enter a whole universe. It's a universe that at the deepest core is very similar to our own—filled with pain, fear, desire and hope. What beautiful treasure waits for the breaking open of your heart?

I want my heart to break open again and again.

✥

The heart that breaks open can
contain the whole universe.

Joanna Rogers Macy

No matter where you live, there are trees somewhere around you. Do you just take them for granted, or do you take the time to notice their life force? Each tree continually changes. Some change to greet the seasons. Others just continue to find their way according to the climate and their nature. We humans are all like that, aren't we?

Adopt a tree and see. Don't pick just any tree, but one whose personality, shape and location really speak to the two of you. Observe its life. You can't always see the changes taking place. Indeed, just like yourselves, sometimes it seems as if change just won't appear. But the tree is forever changing.

And then, suddenly, there it is! Sap running. Buds being born. Leaves and flowers gracing your world. Your tree flexible and strong, bending with the wind. Resilient against the cold. Always heading for the light. Just like the two of you!

**It will be fun for us to adopt a tree
and see ourselves in it.**

&

*We adopted an old tree that's near our home.
Whenever we walk by, we always see the life that's in it
and it makes us think about living with greater force.*

Art Klein and Pat Feinman

No doubt, you're concerned about society. Human suffering touches you deeply and you wish you could do something to help. But you feel powerless. The situation seems overwhelming. War, violence in the schools, child abuse. What can you do?

There is only one thing that can truly heal the world, and that is love. You are not powerless. Everywhere you go, you can pass on your care, smiling and speaking respectfully with even strangers. Give your gratitude generously: Show your appreciation to the shoe repairman, the crossing guard, the airline pilot, the trash collector—anyone who helps you live well. Give to those in need and give with generosity and love. Whenever possible, make your giving personal—face to face with someone who can receive you. With someone who can be healed a bit by connecting with you. With someone who can touch your soul by their expression of gratitude. Love like the world depends on it. It does!

My love helps heal the world.

Healing the world will be brought about through love.
What can I do today to heal the world?

Laurie LeClear

Women and men contain such dark and dreary uncon-scious pools of fear and distrust of one another. It's a wonder their fierce attraction maintains. Yet it does. And when the barriers are brought down through honest, open conversation, it seems a miracle.

Yet, by their silence, so many couples actively create barriers and obstacles to love. "Oh, well, he doesn't need to know about that" and "What difference does it make if I don't tell her about this" are joined together in feeding their fear of each other. They may not be conscious of what they're doing, but their love suffers for it.

Provided you're both committed, you can dissolve most barriers simply by talking with each other. So speak up! Let your spouse know what's going on. Don't harbor secrets. Keep the dialogue open and easy. If need be, you can look for new ways to open up conversation that appeal to you both. Just breaking the ice can be enough to get your love flowing again.

I can dissolve obstacles to love just by speaking up.

But it is nothing short of a revelation to discover
what personal obstacles dissolve when one tries
to speak to another person.

Jacob Needleman

Are you worried about getting rejected? So many people are. Yet, it doesn't really happen the way you imagine. Think about it. If your lover looks at another person in a restaurant and you feel rejected, did your lover reject you by finding someone else attractive? No. You did it. All your lover did was turn to survey the scenery. You immediately felt less than the "scenery" and assumed you were being rejected.

No one can reject you but you! Oh, he might think he'd prefer someone else or she can think it will be easier with another. But those statements aren't about you. They describe the other person's perspective. If your spouse tells you you're unattractive, are you? No, unless you think so.

You can't get hooked by rejection unless you've got the other half of the hook already rotating around inside you. Don't give others the power to reject you. Remove the internal voice that makes you unacceptable in your own eyes. Reject rejection!

I am the only person who can reject me.

I am anal-retentive. I'm a workaholic.
I have insomnia. And I am a control freak.
That's why I'm not married. Who could stand me?

Madonna

When you live together, you inevitably discover very many tender, wounded and fragile places within one another. You automatically know to be really caring in response, right? That's what common sense would tell you. But there's a major obstacle to being gentle and openhearted.

To the degree you're caught up in romantic fantasy about your lover, that's the degree to which you'll have trouble loving your partner's vulnerabilities. You married a strong, protective man or a woman who's sophisticated and independent, right? So when your spouse's fear, insecurity, depression or anger come to the surface, where does your openhearted love go? Into hiding, most likely, and covered over by disappointment and irritation.

Your spouse's vulnerabilities are the best invitation God can send to help you love with all your heart. Remember that you, too, can be very vulnerable, so develop your compassion. Care fully for your mate's tenderness. It's a trust of your own love for your spouse when you are so exposed. Be worthy of that trust.

I tenderly respond to my spouse's hurt places.

≈

Once you become aware of your lover's vulnerabilities,
you have a special responsibility to handle them with care.

Riki Robbins

Confrontation gets a bad rap, as if it's always hostile or even violent. But that's not true. If you can't confront your spouse with the ways he sabotages himself at work, hides her competence from her parents, insists on remaining an adolescent boy, hides her beauty behind self-hating vanity, then how can you ever really be loving, much less useful to each other?

Loving confrontation is one of the gifts of intimacy. Because you're too close to the issue, your spouse can point out your shadow stuff—stuff you can't see. Do you see? It can be the way you kowtow to your boss, roll your eyes in contempt or try too hard to please. Loving confrontation is never meant to put you down. Quite the contrary. When your spouse has your best interests at heart, then it hurts to see you selling yourself short.

When either of you spots a shadow behavior, make sure there's loving agreement to speak up, confront and set one another free.

**I commit to being shown
my shadow side and vice versa.**

❧

*To confront a person with his own shadow
is to show him his own light.*

Carl Jung

When we speak of a faithful spouse, we refer to never straying sexually. But what about all the other strayings—when you forget important dates, show up late, bad-mouth your spouse to friends, or lie about spending or how you use your time? Any of these behaviors and countless more are also acts of unfaithfulness. Why? Because you are cheating, you aren't being faithful to your love.

You may think what your spouse doesn't know "won't hurt him," or "she'll never notice." But you know you're not being faithful. Inevitably a coolness will come between you, and love will gradually be edged out the door.

Commit to being faithful to your marriage—in all ways. If you give your word that you'll do something, do it. If you suspect your behavior may hurt your spouse, rethink what you're doing. If you have trouble remembering important dates, put them in your calendar. Be faithful to love and it will repay you countless times over.

I commit to being faithful to my love.

⤳⤳

*I could never think well of a man's intellectual
or moral character, if he was habitually
unfaithful to his appointments.*

Nathaniel Emmons

There is no one way to see reality. As soon as you understand that you always see life filtered through who you are, and the same is true for your spouse, it will save you a world of heartbreak. You can stop fighting about what is "the truth." You will no longer need to agree on everything. In fact, you will come to enjoy the very different perspectives you each bring to the table.

When you learn to value these differences, you can see that each of you is truly fascinating and wonderfully complex—just the stuff that will keep you curious, eager to learn more about the beguiling, one-of-a-kind mystery that you married!

Practice verbalizing your perspective as just that—yours. "I see it . . . this way." "I understand it to be . . . so-and-so." Then you avoid sounding like God on high who has the truth. You stay open to the perspective of your spouse, and you enjoy the magic of differences.

**My spouse and I see life through
our own distinct perspectives.**

We don't see things as they are, we see them as we are.

Anaïs Nin

No matter how much you love your spouse, there's always room for improvement. Right? Right. Now, how do you make your requests for change in a loving manner? And how do you counteract the defensiveness that may come your way, in objection to your pleas?

Making demands doesn't work, because there's no room for your spouse's reality, only yours. A demand insists that your lover become you. Forget about it. However, making suggestions, inviting discussion, that's much more respectful of both of you and will bring the results you're looking for.

It works best if you agree that you'll both be making suggestions for change. And you'll do it in the most loving way possible. It will often have to be negotiated. Also understand that change won't necessarily be automatic or instantaneous. Finally, agree that you'll be clear if an issue is nonnegotiable. Remember, suggesting change goes both ways. Now, make a suggestion!

I will suggest change, not demand.

To know how to suggest is the great art of teaching.

Ralph Waldo Emerson

Singing together can be very romantic, intimate and fun. It doesn't even matter if you can carry a tune or not. The point is to have a good time singing to and with each other, while strengthening your trust—entertaining yourselves on long road trips, in the shower as an ensemble act or while you're doing the dishes. You can make up your own lyrics to tunes you both know, sing the old standards or even sing along with CDs or tapes you enjoy.

You might go out to karaoke places, go on stage, sing into a microphone and entertain the crowd. On the other hand, you might want to make singing a more serious part of your life and join a church choir or a local singing group, which would include rehearsals and scheduled performances.

The fun of singing together is that it provides another way to be expressive and vulnerable with each other—even if it's just humorous. Don't worry about your voice, just give in to the urge to belt it out!

I get a kick out of our singing.

I had no inborn sense of rhythm;
I couldn't count a thing.
I wasn't singing great at all.

Lena Horne

How much time do you spend on mindless entertainment, surrounded by crowds of people or in some other way distracted from your relationship? Compare this with the time you spend really being together, getting to know and see each other.

We marry for love. We marry for life. And then we spend endless time turned away from one another, as if we no longer find each other fascinating. Oh, yes, there are the demands of work, home and family. True. But what about all the time we avoid intimacy by watching television, gossiping or otherwise "wasting time"? We seem to be so nervous and awkward about being truly intimate, even with those we marry. Are we that frightened of being known and seen? What happens when we see the miracle of our spouse's unique and special humanity?

Today, take the time to really look at your partner. Notice the subtle moods, the particularities known only to you, the depth of the precious person you love. See your love!

Today I consciously see my lover.

❧

*Television has proved that people will look
at anything rather than each other.*

Ann Landers

You probably never aspired to climb Mount Everest. Maybe you've never challenged yourself in major ways. Yet you want a love that lasts forever, that encircles your heart and those around you. You want a life that wakes you up each morning, greeting you with the promise that life is worthwhile. It's worth getting up!

The scared child in you often appeals for things to be easy. No demands or difficulties. Smooth sailing all the way. But adult loving isn't like that. Its sacred promise urges you forward, to grow, to move into higher consciousness, to develop more awareness of yourself and your partner. When you refuse the challenge, you'll feel depressed and anxious. You'll know something is missing in your life. Every day accept that challenge, to open your spirit, to climb into the higher light of love.

Today, know that you are an expression of God's radiance. Know too that as you give wisely and generously, radiance shall be yours forever.

Today I climb higher on my loving path.

Our way is not soft grass, it's a mountain path with lots of rocks.
But it goes upwards, forward, toward the sun.

Ruth Westheimer

Some of the sweetest moments you can share belong to your earlier years, the years when, perhaps, you were shy, acne-faced and terrified to raise your hand in class. Or maybe your spouse tells you about the time he wandered away from home at the age of two, was found by the police "supervising" a new construction project and then punished. Those childhood memories come with you.

Join together to celebrate your shared, sometimes painful, sometimes funny memories—with compassion and acknowledgment for how resilient you both are. You may want to use your childhood nicknames to refer to those precious children, or you may now have cute names to give them. Make them cherished members of your family.

Listen to the dreams of your younger selves. Take pride in all they survived, all they accomplished. Rejoice in all that you've become with those early beginnings. Honor them by being all that you can be—together.

**Today I honor the awkward,
insecure kids we used to be.**

I was dorky longer than I care to remember.

Diane Sawyer

When you think about your own integrity, what do you value? Honesty? Responsibility? Kindness? Loyalty? Generosity?

It's only through your integrity and the integrity you perceive in your partner that you can develop trust and security with one another. Without a solid sense of one another's character, your wedding vows mean nothing. You can never rely on your love or monogamous commitment. Pay close attention to your own sense of integrity. Do your words mean what you say? Are you willing to work for what you want? Or do you find yourself trying to slip around the corners, hoping to not get caught—even in your own eyes?

When your lover affirms your principles and your integrity, that's a very fulfilling form of intimacy. You are recognized at your core as a supremely worthy and valuable person.

Integrity is essential to loving well.

I seek to attain in your eyes
the same integrity that I attribute to you.

Roger Scruton

Being aggressive often gets a bad rap in our society, as if aggression is only abusive. But to be aggressive can also mean to be enterprising, to have initiative, to be active and bold. It's more forceful than being assertive, and sometimes very necessary when you go after what you want or need to stick up for yourself.

So much confusion in relationship originates from our fear of being too aggressive. We could save ourselves so much disappointment and heartbreak if we would all just show up in the straight-out truth of ourselves. And sometimes that means being positively aggressive.

Be aggressive about the importance of your career or protecting your child. Be aggressive about sticking up for yourself if your date or mate mistreats you, ignores you, or holds you second to his parents or her children. Be fully alive. Respect yourself. Don't be afraid to be aggressive when you need to be!

I will practice being more positively aggressive.

*I realized that people would take advantage of
you if you didn't stand up for yourself.
I had to learn to be aggressive.*

Whitney Houston

Perhaps you've been together for quite a while and you've been through a lot together. It's so easy to presume that you know all there is to know about your spouse. You even start making significant decisions without checking to see what your spouse thinks or wants. You're sure you already know. But you can't know. Unless your partner is a one-dimensional character who refuses to learn, grow and be penetrated by life, you will have closed your heart by presuming to know.

If your relationship is healthy, you're both learning and growing, both individually and together. And since your partner is not you, being curious about how she feels or what he wants is one of the wisest ways to avoid presuming you know what's right for both of you.

Today, pay attention to any time you presume to know about your spouse. Then get curious. Ask to know more about issues you're "certain about." Be prepared to learn things you've never known before.

I will learn about my partner rather than presume to know.

❧

Don't ever think you know what's right for the other person. He might just start thinking he knows what's right for you.

Paul Williams

"For richer or for poorer." You've heard that traditional wedding vow many times. But did you believe it for yourself? Many people don't. In fact, cynicism about love may block any possibility of love showing up. When that's the case, some people trade their heart's desire for a fancy lifestyle.

But your car can never comfort you after a scary nightmare. Your pool table can't dance with you in the moonlight. And your engagement ring won't ever be able to make you laugh. The material things in life can be quite wonderful. But if they are a replacement for the emotional love and intimacy you desire, they can never be enough. Your unfulfilled longings will still be there, translating themselves into an endless demand for more, better and bigger.

Today, open yourself to what money cannot buy: the emotional connections you have with people in your life. Most especially, open to the irreplaceable value of feeling the loving connection with your spouse.

**I will make love more important
than material things.**

*The biggest pitfall of ... society is materialism—
people wanting more and bigger and better.*

Laura Innes

You used to feel insecure, fearful and alone. Right? Then when you started dating, those feelings got really bad, often contaminating any chance for real love. Remember? Being different from your date felt terrible. When your date was not like you—that was intolerable. Where was this magical romance you read about and saw in the movies? The bliss that would set you free?

The only way those old feelings go away is by outgrowing them. Your lover—by being different from you and holding a more positive belief about your value than you do—can help you outgrow the past. For this to happen you need to trust that your spouse's endearments, expressions of love, compliments and gifts are a true and accurate reflection of who you really are now. Believe it!

Today, consciously take in everything positive that comes to you. Believe it, if only for a moment. Try it on. See who you really are, as you outgrow your past.

I am outgrowing who I used to be.

I didn't belong as a kid, and that always bothered me.
If only I'd known that one day my differentness would be an asset,
my earlier life would have been much easier.

Bette Midler

B ottom line: love is a choice. Success at love is a continual choice to succeed at love. Yes, there's attraction, sexual passion, fun and enjoyment. But it still comes down to your decision. Do you decide to make love a success? Or do you doom it to failure by choice?

You may be thinking this sounds too scientific, like physics. It is. It's the power of metaphysics, your power to determine how you will feel and behave. And it's part of the metaphysical, scientific, lawful universe that we all live in. You may argue that your last relationship failed, yet you had total positive determination. That may have been true, but did you pick someone who also wanted to be there? If not, in the picking, you voted your no-confidence.

Make sure you and your partner are committed to succeed at love. Then, no matter what comes up you can count on yourselves to be there to do the lovework. And you will succeed.

I consciously choose to succeed at love.

∞

If you believe you can or believe you can't,
you're right.

Henry Ford

October

We grow up never questioning what is unquestioned around us.

MARGARET MEAD

A shorthand definition of intimacy is "In-to-me-you-see." We need to add "and vice versa." Unless intimacy is a two-way street, it can't be fulfilling because that's not intimacy. It's a dead end.

As our lives evolve, we tend to move away from the necessities of mere survival, when "doing" is a primary value, toward a time when "being" is most valued. We find ourselves wanting to be known, through and through, by at least one person—and to be loved for all that we are. And we want to know and love that person in just the same way.

Here's a practical definition of intimacy: "I tell you about me, what's going on inside of me, not because I'm frightened, not because I have a need to be in the spotlight, but simply because I want you to know me." When both of you accept and practice this definition, you will continually be open to intimacy, to more and more of the beauty of truly being known.

I continually open myself to deeper intimacy.

For human beings the more powerful need
is not for sex, but for intimacy.

Rollo May

Do you ever feel possessed by forces that seem outside your control? It may be a snit about losing your favorite sweater, a migraine that attacks during a big project or even an insistence that your spouse celebrate your birthday in just a certain way. No flexibility. No reasoning. Possessed.

When you're possessed, it's not by an exotic extraterrestrial, but by a deep-seated unconscious attachment to some kind of fear. In order to counteract it and keep it in the furthest recesses of your awareness, you developed perfectionistic, even superstitious ways to conduct your life. When any of this gets disturbed, the fear rises, unbidden, and takes over with fierce authority. And you're possessed.

Your spouse may be helpless when this happens. But you aren't. Know that it is fear. When you settle down enough, you can work to change your loyalties from a defense against fear to a vital liveliness. Possession is an invitation to set yourself free!

I release possession by projects, people and things.

If we are possessed by our things or our projects—
our way of doing things—we become captive to them.

Robert E. Wagoner

We've all made mistakes in love. We've all been cruel and we've all had our hearts broken in the name of love. Many of us ended up divorced. Let's face it, there's no way to love without making mistakes.

Mistakes are simply proof that we're living life as fully as we can, not playing it so safe we never fall over the line. We cannot learn if we don't make mistakes—and loving well is all about learning. Think about all you wouldn't understand about yourself, the other sex or marriage if you had never made a mistake. Mistakes of the heart are just evidence of your desire to love more fully.

Today, give yourself praise for all the risks you've taken in love. Give thanks for all that you've learned. And open your heart to all the mistakes still to come as you expand your ability to love more fully, more freely.

I value the mistakes I've made.

❧

Show me a person who has never made a mistake
and I'll show you somebody who has
never achieved much.

Joan Collins

You keep silent, fudge the truth, lie—so you can't be known, you won't be found out. "If you really got to know me, you'd. . . ." What? Reject me, laugh at me, beat me?

Like so many people, withholding yourself may be such a habit that you no longer have access to the reasons you started hiding in the first place. What you do know is that it makes you feel weaker, less than, always stumbling to put forward a "good image." What a drag!

Commit to no longer cheating on love. And with each emotionally naked move toward your lover, you will run into feelings similar to those that caused you to go underground: fear, anxiety, self-doubt, insecurity, sadness, anger, disappointment. Hiding them may have protected you from pain earlier in life, but now you can rescue them and the true beauty of your Self. Respect these feelings and insist that your spouse do the same. No withholding. Only love. Do you promise?

I honestly show my partner who I am.

Something we were withholding made us weak,
Until we found it was ourselves.

Robert Frost

Money is power. Whoever makes it more often controls it. Despite the women's movement, many women still undercut themselves in their marriages by "being taken care of" by their man. Some say they want to "look up to their man." But if they're looking up, in what direction are the men looking?

The more a marriage is based on equality, the more likely both people will feel fulfilled. When one of the partners feels powerless, then they have to resort to underhanded methods of wielding power—passive-aggressive maneuvers to get their way. Chronic resentment, divisiveness and power struggles usually lead to divorce because it's no fun for either person.

Do both of you have a source of income? If not, why not? If you're a stay-at-home mom, you have an important and demanding job. Do you share equally in your husband's earnings as payment? Remember, money is power. Make sure both of you have some of both.

I respect that we both have money.

*If there is to be any romance in marriage,
women must be given every chance to earn a decent living.
Otherwise no man can be sure he is loved for himself.*

Rebecca West

Having versus Being. That's the conflict. It's always our obsession with the material world of Having that leads to wars. On the other hand, it's always the soul urge of Being that brings peace, whether it's in international relations or your marriage.

No doubt you've wondered why bad things happen to you. What if you view these events as necessary, the dissolution that's required to break down old, defensive thoughts and feelings—the dissolution of the ego's attraction to appearances and material possessions as your soul awakens to the illusions it has embraced? The worse these attachments, the worse the pain of dissolution seems to be, so you can be reduced to your most basic components.

Today, consciously surrender your attraction to material possessions and tune in to the passion in your soul—to reveal your true, loving essence.

**For this day I relinquish my attraction
to material possessions.**

&

*If there is to be any peace
it will come through being, not having.*

Henry Miller

Endearing nicknames speak volumes. They claim personal, insider's turf. They're usually playful. And they convey your private intimacy in public. Do you think nicknames are just for kids? Well, when used to convey love, nicknames are a form of flirting. So if you don't like what your spouse calls you, insist on a new nickname.

If you want to create verbal love handles, play with what you know about one another. For example, he likes Foster's Lager, so you call him "Foster" when you want to party. She's crazy for oat muffins, so you call her "my little oat muffin." You turn your differences into a joined name like "SMART"—because one of you is intellectual and the other is an artist.

Have fun playing with inside jokes, terms of affection, any intimate nickname, anything that can be a loving endearment. It might last only for awhile, it might stick around forever. Either way it's a tender and private way for love to pass back and forth between you.

I enjoy flirting by using nicknames.

In our early exuberant and powerful love,
we called each other "Sweetie," which gave way to "Weetie,"
and sometimes, "Weets" or "Weeters." After thirteen years, it
still feels weird to use our first names. May it ever be so!

Don and Paige Marrs

"That's not normal." "What would the neighbors think?" "Who do you think you are!?" The scare tactics of "normal." And to some degree we've all bought into wanting to belong with the "normal." Even if you've had the courage to stand apart, there's still some discomfort, right? Like you could still get caught and be sent to the principal's office?

But look around. Really look around. Normal is not doing so well. Largely unconscious, normal refuses to wake up from the dream of living "like all the rest." Normal keeps refusing the power of self-definition and self-love.

Your life and your love require that you wake up even more than you already have. In fact, the world needs you to be more awake, needs you to renounce "normal" in favor of conscious, independent awareness. Normal loves in clichés. But you can love in realms that echo the light of God's love. Choose wisely.

I want to be anything but normal.

⁂

Society ... educates children to lose themselves
and to thus be normal. Normal men have killed 100,000,000
of their fellow normal men in the last fifty years.

R. D. Laing

"Don't ask, don't tell" is a motto for people who fear their spouse knowing what they were like in the past. But this is a contract from hell. Why? Because imagining what you don't know is more often far worse than knowing the truth. Plus, you miss the intimacy of knowing one another's history, the back story for who the person is today.

Get real. Everybody has a past, some more colorful than others. But if love is going to prevail, you have to release your pasts from jail. You both have had previous loves, you've experimented with all kinds of stuff and you no doubt aren't a faultless individual today.

So, open up your histories and be loved. For that to happen, you both have to be safe recipients for one another's pasts. Otherwise the drifty stuff is in danger of getting attacked, and that's not loving or kind. Love well. Love it all!

I accept that we've both drifted in the past.

I used to be Snow White, but then I drifted.

Mae West

How often do the two of you debate serious issues? Not just disagree with one another, but actually explain your independent positions. Perhaps you expect it would lead to a fight. Well, it could if you need to have the same lockstep opinion. But what if you both want to learn about each other's ways of thinking? Then you could respect your unique points of view, and it would be fascinating to explore each other's logic.

Get to know each other's thoughts about controversial issues: reincarnation, heaven, hell, legalizing drugs, abortion, the death penalty, sex education in schools, doctor-assisted dying, anything you find important. The goal is not to change each other's minds, but to practice thinking out loud and get to know each other more intimately.

Make a discussion date. Pick an issue (maybe you'll each read up on it beforehand) and then take turns explaining your position. Ask lots of questions. Learn from each other. And have a good time!

Thinking is one of the paths to intimacy.

*At a time when "consciousness raising" is
at least relatively popular, thinking itself has enlisted the
support of few defenders, even though it is one of the
chief means of raising one's consciousness.*

Steve Allen

When your spouse does something dumb, breaks a dish or forgets a dentist appointment, your first impulse is to be critical, isn't it? You're upset so you want to set things right and make sure it doesn't happen again. Okay, but what about how your spouse is feeling—standing there blatantly revealed as clumsy or forgetful? Do you take the time to remember what it feels like to be in your lover's shoes?

We've all done plenty of dumb stuff. And we've all been criticized, shamed and punished for it. But how often has anyone put their arms around us with comfort and understanding, warmly assuring us that what happened was no big deal? Reassuring us that we're still loved and that the dish can be replaced, the dentist appointment rescheduled?

Offer your support and compassion instead of criticism when you can. Help yourself by remembering that your spouse's feelings are more important than a dish. That's a gift from your heart and it's real romance!

I will offer support rather than criticism.

❧

*Today, who needs your love and support
rather than your criticism?*

Ruth Cortez

Your body can be a very good Geiger counter for pre- tense. When you're living in integrity, not pretending to be, but genuinely earnest and humble in giving and receiv- ing love, your body will generally hum along pretty nicely. But when you pretend to be "fine" by ignoring the truth— burdened by too much work, shamed by unwanted sexual- ity or sick unto death of your in-laws coming by all the time—your body will issue a physical report card.

Grade C-sized headaches and recurrent colds are putting you on notice that you'd better shape up or you'll be sent to the doctor's office. D-sized recurring accidents and sub- stance abuse alert you that the paramedics are on their way. F-sized catastrophes like heart attacks and cancer can not only land you in the hospital but they announce that life as you've known it will have to change—immediately.

Listen to your body. Get to know it well. Let it guide you to nothing but As and Bs.

**I respect signals from my body
that I am out of synch.**

When one is pretending the entire body revolts.

Anaïs Nin

L ove is not enough. While your love may be immense, it needs your conscious attention to create the fullness of your marriage. Why? Because your relationship is made up of two very different people. Love, by itself, can't know all the ways it will have to form itself to fit who you are and who your spouse is. It must have your navigational skills to keep it on course.

Your conscious attention requires studied care and concern for the health and well-being of your relationship. It's the intellectual, intuitive and emotional navigational equipment that must accompany the flight pattern of your love in order for it to stay on target—and bring it back when it strays off course.

Without conscious attention, you'll take too much for granted. Or you'll expect more than love can ever provide. With your conscious, attentive piloting, you can make love a generous, daily exercise in navigating your precious interpersonal space.

I will consciously attend to my love every day.

But we become disillusioned with love of all kinds
when that care is lacking the element
of conscious attending.

Jacob Needleman

When you think of passion, do you just think of sex? If so, you're cheating yourself. And you're cheating your own sexuality. Why? Because truly sexy people are passionate about their lives, not just orgasms.

If you tend to live a tepid life—reluctant to ride on a whim, shriek with delight, sing in your car or cry with rage, or you otherwise hold back from life—you're missing out on a lot. And so is the person you married.

From this day forward, commit yourself to living your passion. Just little by little, let go of your inhibitions, your fear of permitting others to see how beautiful you are. You will choose to do it in your way, of course, and in your time. You were put here to live. Do it with intensity, with the depth of your being. Then your spouse will have so much more to love, and you will grace the world with who you truly are. We need your passion!

I will live my life with passion.

ⅆ

Passion is attractive!

Matthew McConaughey

Life can be difficult. In fact, it can be very difficult and very painful. Sometimes it's overwhelming—when you survive a tragedy or the death of a beloved. How could God have made life so distressing? It can seem so unfair.

Yet, we have the power to save ourselves from bitterness and despair, from a lifetime of hellish misery—through love. Only through love are we saved. It is in the transcendent forces of love that we find a kind of alchemical heat and pressure that forces us to develop deeper compassion for ourselves and for all others. It is in the embrace of love that we are tenderized, our consciousness expanded beyond the material world. We learn to see life through the heart.

The siren call of romantic fantasy is the promise that you will be saved. And so you shall—after you outgrow the fantasy, survive the disappointment and evolve into the realms of the spirit of real romance and true love.

The salvation of my everyday life is love.

Love is the ultimate and highest goal to which man can aspire.
The salvation of man is through love and in love.

Viktor Frankl

You may not think of yourself as spiritual. The idea of your soul or your essence may be foreign to you. But even if they're familiar, imagine giving yourself fully to these experiences and notice what you feel: watching gold and orange fish swimming in a beautiful koi pond; looking into the eyes of a youngster bright with glee; convincing your boss that you deserve the promotion and large raise; holding your lover close as she weeps in grief, as he prays for a friend in surgery; fighting to save your home from a nearby fire; savoring every bite of strawberry cream pie.

Whatever part of you entered into and gave yourself over to these imaginary experiences—that is your essence, your spiritual core. That is the part of you that is willing to know God through your everyday encounters with your Self.

The most beautiful and true part of you is your essence. Share it with those who will love you well. Make sure you are one of them. Are you one of them?

I live as an expression of my essence.

Our essence is spiritual.
Most of the time we hide our essence from others.
But don't hide your spiritual self from yourself.

Melody Starr

Most people know that good communication is required to create a solid marriage. But many people try to fake it, mouthing terrific words they read in a book or learned from a counselor. But the words signify nothing because they have no heart behind them, no love.

One of the most loving things you can do is speak the truth when you feel distant or flat or you don't actually even know what you feel. You see, when true love is present, your words will not sound tinny or false. There will be a sincerity in your message, even if, at the moment, you are not feeling very intimate or close.

Always be sincere in what you say to your partner. Perhaps the ears can be fooled, but not the heart. The heart can hear love, even when the feeling of love is absent.

**Good communication
is wanting my lover to understand.**

❧

*Though I speak with the tongues
of men and of angels and have not love, I am as a
sounding brass and a tinkling cymbal.*

The Apostle Paul

Without desire you'd never do much of anything. Yet our society is very mixed up about desire. Some people give it a bad rap, as if it's a sin that will lead you into temptation. Others flagrantly flaunt their desire, giving evidence for caution. But the truth is somewhere in the middle.

We need to feel desire. We need to want. Otherwise there is no passionate connection, no soul-filled impulse for the actions we take, the preparation we make, the commitment we give to following our dreams.

Starting today, do as little as possible on automatic pilot. Tune in to your desire, particularly your soul desire. For example, you may want to make love or play but you have to water the plants. Water the plants not because you have to, but because you want your plants to thrive and continue blessing your life with their sensuous greenery. Then, enjoy the rest of your day in the same spirit of desire.

I nourish my desire for a well-fed life.

❧

All human activity is prompted by desire.

Bertrand Russell

Love is a creation. Oh, yes, at first it may sweep you away, but sooner or later the creative process is required to knit your two lives together. To write the melody and the harmony at the same time. To feel the hand of God spinning a web of blessed dew between your impassioned lips.

You may think you're not creative. But of course you are. Everyone is in some ways. The trick with love and relationship is to trust that you can always find your way, through some creative idea, plan or personal transformation, as long as you don't rush it. Creativity can't be rushed. After all, in the Bible, God took six days to create the world. Certainly you get to take weeks, months and even years to create the changes required to best express your love.

You are creative. Never doubt it. Understand that your marriage is a giant canvas on which the two of you continually paint your love. That's creativity!

In my creativity I can touch the divine.

The great joy of the artist is to become aware of . . .
the resemblance between human creation
and what is called "divine" creation.

Henry Miller

Many people understand "compromise" as the best way to settle a fight. But when you compromise, you give up something you don't want to give up and so does your partner. It may quiet the waters for a time, but the resentment builds up over what you've lost, so the fight is bound to explode again—with a new face on it. For the sake of your love, don't compromise.

When a fight erupts, you're simply in the wilderness of your relationship, trying to resolve something, but looking at it from two different angles. Both of you bring distortion to the issue. That's why you're fighting. But also you both bring creativity.

Rather than compromise, commit to finding a new way to be together that respects both of you and that expands your relationship. Be patient. Some conflicts take time to resolve—and when they are, you've both grown.

I refuse to compromise in order to solve a conflict.

∽

Don't compromise yourself. You are all you've got.

Janis Joplin

On a list of priorities, where would you place your relationship? If you didn't put it either number one or two, why not? Ideally, number one would be you and two would be your relationship. Why? Because everything else in your life follows from you and your marriage, including how well you raise your kids and the success of your work.

When you make your marriage a priority, it opens your desire to nurture the love you share. You want to touch base during the day, just to share what's happening. When you both arrive home, your relationship is important enough to stop anything else you're doing to listen to each other's concerns. When you sense something is off, you'll stop long enough to talk it through, even if one of you doesn't see the need.

Give yourself and your love top billing. Let this conscious choice support the care and feeding of the life you share. Enjoy the desserts as well!

My relationship is my top priority.

We have made our love the top priority in our lives.
And we treasure the results of that choice.

Barbara Steffin and Nick Rath

When you get lost in a heated discussion or passionate fight with your spouse, or when you become confused about your loyalties to your parents versus your marriage, it's very helpful to call upon the services of your Personal Observer. You may not know you have this handy helper, but you do. You just need to become aware of its services.

Your Observer is that part of your mind that stands apart from and watches the situation your personality is caught up in. The Observer has more of an objective perspective, holds your best interests at heart and gives you some straight scoop about the choices you might make. Usually your Observer is right on the money, if you know how to listen.

Right now, as you read this, notice that there is a part of your mind that is watching you, the reader. Check to see what your Observer thinks about you reading this. Got it? Great! You and your Observer are now a team!

I will get to know and use my Personal Observer.

❧

Get in touch with your little observer, a little voice inside you that enables you to detach yourself from what's going on and see the whole situation in perspective.

Riki Robbins

Just because you're friends, lovers, husband and wife doesn't mean you don't have to have separate lives outside your marriage. Even if you work together, even if you enjoy being with each other more than anything, the two of you can never supply each other with everything you'll want from life. Yet, that's what many couples imagine—putting expectations and pressures on their marriage that marriage can never meet.

Which of your friends is available for companionship when your spouse is not? What are your hobbies? What do you enjoy just for fun? How do you serve your community? What do you do to keep yourself intellectually interesting? What do you do that stretches your life beyond your marriage, so that you fulfill yourself and bring back to your spouse someone who is fresh and continually interesting?

Commit yourself to having a life outside your marriage. This way you serve yourself and you serve your marriage.

Everything in my life cannot
come from my marriage.

The trouble with many married people
is that they are trying to get more out of marriage
than there is in it.

Elbert Hubbard

Most of us grew up learning some form of "Put your best foot forward." Did you interpret it to mean never let anyone see you weak or stumbling, never reveal what you really feel unless it's "happy"? Most of us did. That's why we're so uncomfortable with emotional intimacy. We think we're doing something wrong, that we won't be liked, we'll be laughed at or even hated. Just for being ourselves.

But your "best foot" is really the inner guts of your being, not some manicured performance designed to keep everyone at a comfortable distance.

When we build our marriages, we too often leave out those deeper realities, depriving love of the rich mix of emotional colors and textures. Just like crops need fertilizer, your love needs your vast life experience. Laugh, cry, rage, feel ashamed, get anxious, feel afraid, giggle, be joyous, get embarrassed, be bold and on and on. Feel it all! Express it to your partner, never to manipulate, only as a gift to the both of you, to the love you share. That's freedom!

**Love means I have the freedom
to fully express myself.**

≫

*Your tears can form a coursing, raging stream
of freedom for others to sail on.*

Art Klein

Y ou want or need a little time together. And that's all you have—a little time. So, take a "coffee" break, either at home or a local coffee/tea emporium. Enjoy your favorite drinks and share a pot of real romance.

You may have something important you need to discuss, and the cozy time helps set a receptive mood. You may just want to read or do some paperwork—and it's more fun doing it together over tea. Maybe it's just good to get out of the house, and a cup of coffee gives you a welcome break from family duties. Maybe you're just hanging out after a walk or bike ride, relishing being together.

Don't underestimate the magic of a short coffee break together, when you focus on the pleasure of your drink and the beauty of being together—no matter the purpose. It's good to the last drop!

I enjoy our "coffee" dates.

❧

It is very deep to have a cup of tea.

Katagiri Roshi

To help you round off your rugged edges, you need to mix it up with a partner who meets you nose to nose. Someone who's willing to go to the mat for what's important, yet never interested in making you lose. That's exciting, enlivening and spiritually expansive. That's lovework at its finest.

Too often we cheat love by bringing forth pale comparisons of who we really are. We allow mistreatment in the name of love. We fail to be worthy adversaries for one another. Carbon needs heat and pressure to transform into a diamond. Then it must be cut for its true brilliance and value to shine. We humans are no different.

Insist that you and your spouse be good matches for each other. That doesn't mean you fight all the time. It means you're both willing to give as good as it gets. That's exciting. That's a love match.

My partner is a worthy match.

❧

What is exciting is not for one person
to be stronger than the other ... but for two people
to have met their match and they are equally stubborn,
as obstinate and as passionate as the other.

Barbra Streisand

In the beginning of love, it's easy to ignore the stuff that might be a problem. "Who cares," you say to yourself, even if you do notice, because you're filled with such a blissful exuberance for life that nothing else really matters. Then later, in order to keep your marriage on an even keel, you continue to turn away from issues that might rock the boat. But, behind your back, out of direct sight, the boat is taking on water and will soon go under if you don't wake up and open your eyes to reality.

We all know the phrase, "Love is blind." But it's not love that's blind, it's our reluctance to shift out of infatuation into the deep intimacy and real romance of love—through good times and through those that can send out bursts of difficulty. Keep your eyes wide open, searching out the true beauty of it all.

Open yourself to the whole of your relationship, keep your eyes and heart wide open, and do your lovework!

I no longer turn a blind eye to the reality of love.

Nobody should be so desperate that they ignore
big red flags thrown right in their faces.

Cynthia Heimel

We all have such high hopes for romance, for love everlasting. Yet, when we find a relationship that begins to truly open our heart and expand our dreams, it's so easy to find fault, to be disappointed, to wreck it.

Why would we do such a thing? Because we don't know how to focus on the positive, to enjoy what is. All too often, we look through the lens of idealized fantasy, of perfection. Then, when reality doesn't match up, we trash it! But, as humans, we have the enormous power to change our minds, thus changing our point of view so that we can concentrate on the blessings, while we do the lovework required by the inevitable challenges.

Today, focus on loving, on receiving, on enjoying what you're doing—even if it's the laundry, writing a report or working out the budget. Life comes to us on its terms. It's up to us to make the most of it. Don't cheat yourself!

I can change my mind and my point of view.

❧

Some people walk in the rain. Others just get wet.

Roger Miller

Were you taught to strive for perfection? Did it make you think that only the perfect presentation could make you lovable? Maybe you tried to live up to an ideal persona. Perhaps you rebelled. Either way, you never learned the truth about love.

Love can only exist in the humanity of our everyday lives. Even for people who are wealthy or famous, love can only be meaningful for the person they are when the banks are closed and the audience has gone home. In fact, most often we're loved most dearly for the little, idiosyncratic ways we laugh, sneeze and tip our head, drop the keys in the plant by the door. Sure we're admired for our wisdom, brilliance, creativity, values and success in the world—and that's important, too. But it's our humanity that really holds the lock on love.

Today, think about all your spouse's mannerisms and how you'd miss them if suddenly you were widowed. Make sure your sweetheart knows how much you adore those favorite, very human quirks that make your heart smile and dance with joy.

Love celebrates our humanity.

Love that stammers, that stutters, is apt
to be the love that loves best.

Gabriela Mistral

There can be no life without death. For adulthood to come, childhood must die. For spiritual meaning to live, material compulsion must die. We live in a continuous cycle of death and rebirth. Yet, most people deny death and then live deadened by the fear of dying.

How often do you discuss death with your spouse? The possibility of one another's untimely death, the deaths of other loved ones, the death of old identities for new life to enter—any of these topics can lead you to a more profound understanding of one another.

Don't try to escape from death. It's all around you, from the fading grass in your lawn to the family member who recently passed on. It permeates your life as you move from one town to another, move from one job to the next, as you love with a fresh intensity never before experienced. Embrace death and it will bring more life to your love than you've ever imagined.

**Love is made sweeter through
my acceptance of death.**

*When you start using death as a means of focusing on life,
then everything becomes just as it is just this moment,
an extraordinary opportunity to be alive.*

Stephen Levine

The masks and costumes we choose to wear on Halloween probably come closer to who we really are than the straightjackets or clown impersonations we've adopted for everyday wear. Because on Halloween we give ourselves permission to be bold, beautiful, wild, fanciful and clever. The rest of the time, most of us are hidden behind attempts to be "normal" and to "fit in."

But love doesn't know how to get inside you when you're hidden behind masks. It can't go where it's denied. You have to believe that you're lovable for love to show up in your treat bag. You have to make yourself available, by taking off your masks. That way your love won't be a trick.

So, today, enjoy Halloween. But be sure to really give your lover and friends a treat: Go as you are. There's no better gift on this planet than to be allowed inside the true reality of another human. That's a treat.

**My masks don't trick anyone,
so I'll treat them to who I am.**

*Love takes off the masks we fear we cannot live without,
and know we cannot live within.*

James Baldwin

November

*Man must evolve for
all human conflict a method
which rejects revenge, aggression and
retaliation. The foundation of
such a method is love.*

MARTIN LUTHER KING JR.

Love is always looking for a place to settle down. It gets very sad and uncomfortable if there's lots of worrying and complaining about the lack of love when it's right there—so it moves on. It won't stay where it's not wanted and welcomed.

Create an open field of love-catcher energy around you. Now you can't be graspy about it, love needs to know that it's free to stay or go. If it's comfy, it'll stay. If it feels too confined, it'll have to split for the mountains or someplace where it can be free. To make a safe place for love, a love-catcher open space, focus on all that is good in your life. Refuse to give your attention to needless worry or fear. Replace it with appreciating what you already have and what you can accomplish in the moment.

Today, focus on keeping the energy around your body clear of negative debris, opening the way for love to come to you. Be a love catcher!

I will clear the path for the abundance of life.

Turn your thoughts toward the good and pleasant aspects of your life, while letting go of habitual, fearful thinking. It creates an open field around you that draws more and more of the beauty, wonder and magic of life in your direction.

Davina Colvin

Why can't we be satisfied with what we've got? That's a common lament—even among the happily married. Why? Because static satisfaction is the death knell to love's spirit. The energy of love is always in pursuit of more—from you and for you. In many ways it wants more for you than you may even desire. Love is more powerful than you are.

Some people become confused and seek new experience with a new person. Too bad. It's most often a waste of time, unless understood as a wake-up call for both people in the marriage. Stay where you are and seek to find the undiscovered within yourselves, explore the next path in your love. You could call it serial monogamy with the same person, how's that?!

Once love takes over your spirit, you will be always at the command of love's insistence that you stay vitally alive and intimately connected. Rejoice in being a seeker!

I respect that love compels us to seek for more.

❦

Love in its very nature is poetic:
it constantly seeks something other than what is—
it seeks what is new and undisclosed.

Robert E. Wagoner

Compared with love notes, love letters are a more intense form of making love on paper. Because a love letter takes time and thought to compose, you may not be able to write very often. But when you do, pour your heart out to your spouse and let the poetry of your soul sing its song. This is a very romantic and erotic vehicle for opening to new dimensions of your love.

You may want to write by hand. You can send it through the mail and add fun words and symbols—like "correspondence confetti" (available at your stationery store) to enclose with your letters. Or, you can write to your beloved on your computer and send it through e-mail. Just remember that it may not be truly private.

To intensify your intimacy, make love-letter dates. Each of you brings a letter, to which you add candlelight, wine, dessert, whatever would make your evening complete. Then take turns reading out loud the letter written to you—very slowly.

I write love letters to deepen our love.

Write to me ...
And let not the ink serve as a mask.

Manuel Ugarte

337

"Try" is a weasel word. Sounds pretty good if you don't examine it. But under inspection, it's a word filled with wishy-wash. You don't have to commit to anything heart and soul if all you say is "I will try to change," "try to come by," "try to remember."

To be fair, there are times when you can only commit to "trying" to remember something your spouse has asked you to be more sensitive about. In fact, to promise that you will never be insensitive again would be an absurdity. There is the learning curve, after all, and you need time and practice to set new behaviors predictably in place. But a firm resolution would still be that you commit to change and you will strive to remember the very next time.

Become more conscious about how you use the word "try." Do not cheat on yourself by using it to avoid commitment. Take your stand to love more consciously and mean it.

I will do what I say, not "try" to do it.

&

Try? There is no try.
There is only do or do not do.
Yoda, *The Empire Strikes Back*

Some people have a hard time being intimate and affectionate because they think they have to put on a scene from the Royal Shakespeare Theater for it to be sufficiently romantic. But often—in fact, most of the time—all that's needed is a "sweet nothing" whispered in the morning, scribbled on his bathroom mirror, stuck with Post-It notes on her steering wheel.

Whether you whisper that her legs are the greatest, his butt is the best or shout out the punch line to a favorite joke, you're saying "I love you" in very romantic ways. You can continually create sweet nothings that capture the essence of your private intimacies. For example, you're mad that the quilt keeps sliding off your bed and you say, "Ick the Quilt!" Then, "Ick the Quilt" becomes a character in your relationship, an embodied sweet nothing that you share.

Sweet nothings can range from suggestive to playful. What they're saying is "Our relationship is special, I love you."

I whisper sweet nothings to my love every day.

*Love is looking at my darling first thing
in the morning, holding her close and whispering
sweet nothings in her ear.*

Peter Charad

Firirst you project all manner of perfection onto your lover. You're ecstatic! Oops, oh dear, some social gaffe ruined it all. Devastation. Madness beyond redemption. Now you project onto your soon-to-be-former lover every sin you can think of. Chaos! But your so-called lover has never been seen for real. It's all been projection.

Projection is extraordinarily common. It happens every time we see a well-dressed man and assume he's a wealthy businessman (and later learn he's living on credit and owes the IRS) or we see a female cop and assume she's hardened and tough (until we see her at a party, dressed ultra-fem, laughing and having fun). It becomes disastrous in our marriages when we can't see our own faults or our own worth and project it onto our partner. Then we're way out of synch and creating disaster.

Don't project your dark stuff or your gold onto your spouse. Because either way, you're in relationship with illusion. See reality—both of yours!

I want to love my lover "as is."

           ⤫

Because you're not what I would have you be
I blind myself to who, in truth, you are.

Madeleine L'Engle

"If you loved me, you would. . . ." "But I wouldn't have done that. . . ." "Why can't you just do it my way. . . ?" How often do you get caught by the curse of presuming you're identically alike? Blaming each other. Trashing an otherwise fine relationship, just because your spouse did something in a way you never would.

Yet, if you'll just take a serious look at how different the two of you are physically, you might even laugh at your egotism— which is based solely on your self-centered ideas of your partner and vice versa. You are so obviously different from each other—size, weight, hair, skin and eye coloring. Right? Then why on Earth would you imagine that you're going to see the world, and especially the world of love, exactly the same way?

Start each day by really looking at each other, consciously noting how different you are physically. Remind yourself that different function follows different physical form. That will help you to deal with all your differences that day. *Vive la différence!*

I will respect the lessons of our physical differences.

*Our dramatic size differences (he/American well over
a foot taller and she/Thai weighing half as much) actually helped
open us up to the process of ridding ourselves of the
"you should know how I feel" curse.*

Bryan and Narumol Standley

You may imagine that the joy you felt on your wedding day was the best it could get. And some people let their relationship die because all they focused on was the glamour and excitement of the "big day"—the gown, the showers, the gifts, the wedding, the honeymoon. But what if your wedding was just the outer symbol for the abundance that could be yours?

What if your love for each other could continue to grow day after day? What do you love about your spouse? Financial support? Great humor? Hot sex? Tender neediness? Fits of temper? All of the above and more? All of the above, right? Because when you genuinely love someone, you end up loving the whole package, even if you don't like some stuff.

All that's needed for your love to keep growing is for you to keep getting to know each other, with a deepening understanding and respect for your differences. It's very simple. There's simply more to love.

I open myself to grow as we grow.

I've never been in a relationship like this when, truly,
I'm more in love with him today than the day I married him.
I would hear about it but didn't think people really had it.

Michelle Pfeiffer

To be grounded in love is to be grounded in the darkness, not the light. Sound contradictory? But think about it. All new life starts in the dark—babies in the womb, plants underground, inventions in someone's imagination. Our ability to empathize with another's misery originates in the darkness of our own experience. If we attempt to embrace only light, we teeter on the edge of righteous pride, "ooh aah" spirituality and a serious lack of character.

To love only the "good" and "nice" is to love not at all. That's a denial of life's fullness and depth. Make darkness your teacher, the source of humility and grace. When you see your spouse behaving less than elegantly, rather than denying it or punishing, see how love is trying to express itself through the darkness. Perhaps their behavior is an attempt to not be afraid of your judgment.

The light tries to seduce us with illusions of purity, while every dark moment offers the possibility of enlightenment.

I look to the darkness to illuminate the light.

When I was very young I feared the dark,
But now I see it's the more natural state.
We come from an eternity of it,
Blink briefly in the light, and then return.

Steve Allen

When you think of romance, you may imagine breakfast in Paris, or underwater escapades in Hawaii. But what about every day? What about all the moments you connect in a special way—from tender understanding to funny jokes, even your running debate about the correct name of a vegetable—anything that is special to the two of you? What if that is real romance?

Real romance waits for you every day when you stay open to all the ways you touch one another, even when you're apart. Remember this morning when he brought you orange juice or she kissed the back of your neck as you got out of bed? Or yesterday when he hugged your daughter after her team lost, or she called your mom to wish her good luck on the real estate test?

Don't wait for big-deal romance. It's wonderful, to be sure. But every day, real romance is there to give and receive as soon as you open your heart to experience it.

I enjoy the romance of our everyday life.

*She calls a turnip a "sweet" and I keep
saying it's just a turnip. Can you believe that we
have discussions about vegetables?*

Liam Neeson

We would all like to be wealthy and live a comfortable lifestyle. Right? But what does that mean? What kind of wealth would really be satisfying?

You may increase your financial wealth enormously. And that may be satisfying. But, on the other hand, you may live in extravagant abundance, yet suffer from an impoverishment of the soul. When that's the case, God gets very unhappy, because your behavior reflects very poorly on you and God.

God asks you to develop your wealth. God gave you the gift of love. Use this most precious gift wisely. When you do, your love is the greatest gift to God that God can imagine. Give it with grace!

I find my true wealth in my ability to love.

Man discovers his own wealth
when God comes to ask gifts of him.

Rabindranath Tagore

When you marry, when you have a family, you end up being a nurse and sometimes an orderly. You can do it with love or resent every moment of it. Why not make your bedside manner a love offering?

Of course you probably weren't schooled for the job, but when you're needed to change bandages, pull out a splinter or just drive someone to the doctor, you get the call to action just the same. For a great bedside manner, remember to check and see what's really wanted. Some people like lots of attention and plenty of orange juice and chicken soup. Others want nothing more than to have their peace and quiet guarded for dear life.

Give the gift of caretaking with all the courage and heart you can. Be respectful that some things may make you squirm, and your spouse needs to know that, if it makes you awkward with your attentions. But always, what is deeply healing is your love.

I will take care when someone I love is ill.

❦

Watching my husband take care of our sick child made me so proud of how kind he was.

Mary Helen Snow

I t all works really backwards about love, you know. The more you make an effort to be really fascinating, super sexy or intellectually impressive, the less appealing you are. The more you just show up and be who you are, the more people's hearts open and find you irresistible. Weird, isn't it? That's why the rules for catching a guy don't work any better than jumping from planet to planet. No matter what happens in the beginning, you still have to come back to Earth and get on with the real stuff of love.

Your real stuff—when it's transparent, when there's no defensive junk around it—is unbeatable. After all, when you can be transparent your spouse gets to enjoy all your funky humor, dearest tenderness and even your attempts to rewire the lamp.

You bring the light of spring when you're happy and when you're down, your spouse gets to visit the deserts of ancient lands. The whole world is in you—when you're transparent.

**I commit to becoming more
transparent to my spouse.**

*The more we take pride in who we are,
the more transparent we are willing to be.*

Nathaniel Branden

So many people wreck their relationship by putting it on "cruise control," imagining that it will take care of itself. It will stay simple and predictable. No muss, no fuss. But that's the same as planting a garden, landing in the hammock and trusting that God will weed, water and prune.

Joining two distinctly different people's lives together—under the same roof, often even working together, frequently introducing children into the mix—is a very volatile concoction. That's what makes love and marriage so attractive, so compelling. It's a recipe for excitement, for trouble, for bliss and for maturity. Almost anything in life can become part of the ups and downs of a marriage experience. Real-life love invites us to surrender to the fullness of life's adventure, and that always includes ups and downs.

Today, appreciate the stimulation and liveliness of all the ups and downs in your relationship. Notice how boring it would be if it were always the same.

I accept the ups and downs of a real relationship.

※

*I don't know anybody who hasn't gone through
ups and downs in a marriage.*

Whitney Houston

When you were single, you probably thought that seduction would be unnecessary once you were married. Sex would be easy and available anytime you wanted it. Yet, for many couples, once they're committed sex loses its sizzle. Why? Because they no longer seduce one another.

Well, what's the need to seduce after you're both committed? The need lives inside the fear and anxiety about being truly intimate. For marital sex to keep its sizzle, you both need to bring your emotional selves fully into play. That means expressing what you like and don't. It means revealing your fears, embarrassment, shyness and the lusty noise of spontaneous, exuberant orgasm. So there's lots of room for seduction in marital sex, but now it's being seductive enough to entice one another's vulnerable spirits to join you in making love.

Seduce each other into the heart space of sexuality. Get past the tyranny of the orgasm to really find each other.

I will continue learning to seduce and be seduced.

❧

Pursuit and seduction are the essence of sexuality.
It's part of the sizzle.

Camille Paglia

"Pain, shpain. Who wants to wallow in self-pity?! Life's too short to worry over every little disappointment. I'm a positive person. Right?" Wrong! If this sounds anything like you, think again. Because if you can't acknowledge your own pain, you keep yourself a stranger to some of your partner's (and your children's) most tender experiences. You can never be truly intimate. And no one can ever know you well enough to love you.

Life comes with pain. In fact, Buddha said, "All is suffering." It's not the suffering that's the problem, it's how we use it to either indulge in misery and manipulate other people with it, or deny it and keep ourselves cut off from the painful aspects of reality.

Embrace your pain. Learn from it. Enhance your empathy and self-love. Learn from it. Let it move you to change your life. But mostly, let it tenderize your heart so that you can be in your spouse's corner with full empathy when the going gets rough.

**Acknowledging my pain helps me
connect with my lover's pain.**

*If you've never had pain, you
never have empathy.*

Rosie O'Donnell

Reading is highly underestimated as an intimate activity. You can read silently together in the same room, even snuggled in bed, or read aloud to one another. Either way, you're on the same page, open to learning and having fun. Reading can spark humor and laughter, new learning, even the passion of erotic tales. Or you can share your own writing with one another.

Try reading aloud to each other. Make a romantic date out of it. Serve drinks and snacks. Dress sensuously. Sit so you can touch each other. Open your hearts in both your reading and listening. As you hear each other's voices, filled with the passion or humor for a subject, take in the gift of the moment.

What a great, romantic treat to learn about the same subject, laugh at jokes or cartoons, or begin a discussion you could never have expected. Romantic reading—you never know where the worm in the book will take you.

I commit to making time to read together.

Reading aloud to one another is one of the most intimate things a couple can do, especially when they risk their hearts and souls in the reading.

Shatana Roberts

Why does marriage have to be so difficult? Everyone in an intimate relationship struggles from time to time. Okay, so why? All you want to do is get along and have a good time, right? Well, God has bigger plans for you than that and that's why marriage is such a challenge. It's a training ground for spiritual champions. And you signed up for the course!

When life sends your marriage obstacles—you lose your job or somebody sues you—you can give up. Or you can strap on your spiritual breastplate, grab your sword of determination and go tackle the issue. As long as you don't give up, it's bound to make you stronger.

When the two of you get stuck in a conflict, the same thing applies. God is just extending you an invitation to get spiritually stronger, and you need this emotional workout to become more of a champion. Rise to the challenge!

**I understand that life's challenges
make me stronger.**

※

What doesn't kill me makes me stronger.

Albert Camus

If you had been more conscious, more informed about life's true challenges, you, no doubt, would have lived your earlier life very differently. But you didn't know and you didn't see how to do it another way. You were young, after all.

Don't let regret about the past color and contaminate your life in the present moment. If all you can think about is "what might have been," you can never make the choices now that will guarantee a regret-free future. Your life and your relationship need you to be fully present today. "What might have been" is a form of romantic attachment to suffering. Stop it now and get on with living your life.

The only way to make up for the years that are regrettable is to make the years you have left truly unforgettable. Focus on what you love, what you desire. Go after it. Pull out all the stops. What do you have to lose anyway? Only future regret!

I live and love to the fullest with no regret.

When we stop wasteful and idle, useless regretting,
the energy of regret for time wasted
can become a power for good.

Arthur Brisbane

Compassion is the connection and care you feel when you identify with someone else's pain or joy. When your compassion is offered in love, it can turn a devastating disappointment into a time of tender intimacy, grief into shared loss and healing, a success into celebration.

When your spouse feels down, are you able to identify and offer support and care? Or do you insist on an immediate change of mood, because it upsets you? Do you rejoice in your lover's successes or ignore them? Compassion is identified with the experience of the other. When you lack compassion, you're stuck in yourself.

Practice seeing the situation from your lover's point of view. If she scorches your shirt or he breaks your vase, rather than immediately getting angry, remember how awful it feels to make a mistake and ruin something for someone. Offer your loving compassion. (You can express your disappointment later.) The loving, intimate connection you'll feel is far more valuable than any shirt or vase.

I will be more compassionate with my spouse.

I'm just trying to get across the idea
of compassionate connection as a way of life.

Robin Williams

No one had a perfect childhood. Each of us was raised by parents who received no formal training in child rearing. They loved us the best they could within the limitations of their personalities and, for some, the defects of their character. They lacked knowledge about child development and psychological growth of the individual.

For us, their children, this meant that we made do with whatever we got. No matter how much or how little love we got, we survived!

But now that you are in a loving relationship you think of as "family," emotional ghosts may haunt you—turning fights into wars, reducing you to tears over petty slights, magnifying your beloved's flaws and preventing you from receiving your spouse's obvious love. Why? Because old issues from childhood are surfacing—to be addressed and healed. Don't blame your spouse. These wounds belong to your past. Mature love requires that you grow beyond the limitations of your parents.

**I honor my childhood by living
beyond its limitations.**

*It's okay to have wounds from our childhood triggered
as long as there is consciousness in the relationship
to heal it once it has been triggered.*

Alanis Morissette

There is no way to be married without getting hurt. How you react to those hurts will, to a large degree, determine the success of your love. If you experience your wounds as caused by your spouse's calculated viciousness, you can only feel like a helpless victim. But when you see your spouse as someone distinctly different from you, then you can understand that your differences may have just banged into each other. She may have meant no harm. Even if he did, you've probably done the same. Understand, forgive, heal and let it go.

But if you cannot let go, you remain a victim and your spouse is an unloving jerk. If that's true—get a divorce. Immediately. If it's only how you feel, then change your perspective to include the clash of differences, human imperfection and occasional angry outbursts.

Today is a day to do emotional housecleaning. The wounds you're holding on to are garbage contaminating your marriage. Throw them out!

Today I forgive myself and my spouse for past hurts.

※

*To be wronged is nothing unless you
continue to remember it.*

Confucius

I sn't it fun when you both find something funny? When the two of you giggle like kids, or belly laugh at the same thing? Playing and silliness can't be overrated for their power in love.

But what about laughter as "the best medicine" when the frustrations of life get to be too much, when your spouse disappoints you just at a crucial moment? Does that seem impossible? Unrealistic? What if it's not? What if you could throw your hands in the air, remember how much you value your marriage and laugh at the absurdity of it all? What if you could laugh together, knowing you'll have to figure out a solution to the issue? But for now, you could surrender to love's complexity—take a break—and laugh!

Today, open your mind and heart to the absurdity of life's challenges. Give up control, without giving up yourself, and laugh as much as you can. Then you can solve the issues with increased grace and love.

I will find humor in our life.

❧

It's no laughing matter,
but it doesn't matter if you laugh.

Jennie Gudmendsen

At the beginning of a relationship, you may be vital, bold, spunky, speaking up and asserting yourself. Then it gets serious. You want it to last. You don't want to upset the delicious balance you've both created. You hold back, you avoid confronting your partner. You seldom disagree anymore. You become a ghost of your previous self. The person your lover fell in love with is disappearing.

The best way to feel disrespected in a relationship is to make yourself invisible. Oh, you may be strong and powerful at work, but when you get home you avoid ruffling feathers. You avoid your passion and your dreams. Pretty soon, both of you are thinking, "Is this all there is?" Why? Because your spouse no longer respects the woman he married, that woman disappeared. And when you did that, you destroyed your own self-respect.

Today, assert yourself. With respect for your partner, speak up. Ask for what you want. Disagree. Respect yourself and care more for your relationship. Be assertive!

Others will respect me when I assert myself.

Asserting yourself while respecting others is
a very good way to win self-respect.

Janice LaRouche

"Home" often triggers an image of the family at a feast. They may, or may not, be enjoying one another. At one time, a place with an abundance of food would have been a pretty darn good home. But today we want far more than that. We want to sit down in our home and be known, be well understood by at least one person—our spouse.

We want more meaning in our lives. We need our lives to count for something beyond a paycheck or raising a brood of children. We want to have someone know us intimately and say, "I love who you are." For this to happen, we must teach our spouse how to understand our individuality: quirks, brilliance, whims, big heart, fears and triumphs. Not just know about us, but understand.

Make a home together. Take time every day to understand one another. Dig the cellar of understanding and your home will support and comfort you both for all your years.

I will make our marriage a home.

Home is not where you live, but
where they understand you.

Christian Morgenstern

L ove loves to be celebrated! One of the easiest ways to honor love is to create rituals that express who you are together. Rituals instantly reconnect you after a time apart, remind you of all that you've been through together and join you in creative, unique fun!

Many events of your daily life can be enhanced by ritual. Bedtime, mealtime, holidays, birthdays, triumphs, travel, grief, anything. A ritual is simply something you agree to do at a certain time. Toast each other at dinner with a daily compliment. Photograph vacations for a memory book. Say a private, candlelit eulogy for any loss. Enjoy a weekend get-away for each of your birthdays. Donate money to a charity on your anniversary. At bedtime with your kids, make up silly stories about family members.

Get creative. Enjoy each other's ideas. Try them out. Change them. Make your life together as fun, romantic, silly, sentimental and meaningful as you can with rituals that express your love.

**I will help us create rituals that
celebrate and honor our love.**

∾

*Creating meaningful personal rituals throughout the day
eliminates the dullness of routine, enriches and elevates the events
of our lives, and at the same time comforts us.*

Alexandra Stoddard

How often do you say "thank you" to your spouse? How often do you feel grateful for the loving kindness, consideration and partnership that is given to you? Or do you take it all for granted—as if it just comes with being married?

Loving comes in so many forms. It's in the hard-won pay-check, in sticking to the monthly budget. It's in washing the car and bathing the baby. It's in every gentle caress and every resolved fight. To enhance the splendid complexity and richness of your everyday experiences together, you can transform them into extraordinary intimacy. Very simply, you have the ability to feel grateful and to express your gratitude—openly and often.

Today, take nothing for granted. Stay aware of all that you are thankful for. Even if some things may be difficult, irritating or annoying—remember, without the sand in an oyster, you never end up with the pearl. Express your grati-tude! Say thank you!

I am thankful for all the blessings of my relationship.

If the only prayer you say in your whole life
is "thank you," that would suffice.

Meister Eckhart

Many people believe that to create a lasting marriage, you must sacrifice yourself, that you are obligated to please your spouse no matter what it costs you emotionally or spiritually. Not only is this a recipe for divorce, it's also a good way to end up an emotional disaster. Love never demands belittling obligation or demeaning sacrifice. Love never intends to put you down. Never.

Love waits for the gifts of your heart to be given and received with grace and true desire. Love is patient, knowing that the heart opens gradually, only when it knows it is safe and that its overflowing will be joined in warm embrace.

Listen only to the call of love's journey. Refuse to spoil the dance and lose your way. Today, do only what your heart sincerely desires to do. Express only what love wants to speak. Receive all that is given in return. Enjoy!

I will do nothing today out of obligation.

*Never do anything in relationship
out of a sense of obligation.*

Neale Donald Walsch

Caught up in romantic fantasy, we imagine that beyond twenty-something we're no good for love. We paint illusions of the perfect life—on the ski slopes, dancing in clubs, no wrinkles, no flab. We fear our spouse will go look for someone younger, someone sexier. It's easy to believe that wild partying and wild sex are all that matter—and you're too old for that stuff.

But in real life you're always capable of becoming more appealing, more exciting. Age works for you, not against you. The expression of your character only gets wiser, more fascinating and more clearly drawn with life experience. Study, learn, respect your own opinion, voice it. Stay alive. Relish the full breadth of life experiences that are yours. That way you are never bored or boring.

Take pride in the years you have lived. Value the character that shows in your face. Offer yourself to your spouse like a good bottle of wine—to be tasted slowly for as long as possible.

I am aging like fine wine.

I believe your age is totally how you feel.

Joan Collins

N ever, never give up on yourself! It wastes your life and teaches people not to love you.

No matter how you've lived your life, you always have the power to discover more about who you can be and how you want to live. You are the architect of your journey here. Don't get stuck and stay there because it seems too frightening to change. It's actually far more frightening to never change. And besides, love can only find its way into your heart if you are finding yourself.

What are you afraid you'll find if you open up to discover more about what you want out of your marriage? Out of life? Perhaps you'll have to grieve over wasted years. That's okay. Most people need to do that. Afraid you might wreck your safe, predictable marriage if you start rocking the boat? Maybe. But more than likely you'll breathe life into immense possibilities for both of you.

It's never too late to discover who you are and how to be more loving. Commit to it today!

It's never too late to discover myself.

The delights of self-discovery
are always available.

Gail Sheehy

December

*The process of maturing
is an art to be learned, an effort
to be sustained.*

MAYRA MANNES

Think back to a time when you were suffering and alone. When you had no idea who to turn to, how to get your life back on track. And then something happened, someone came into your life and you were different. Somehow, some way, God managed to bring you a spark of hope, insight or love. With that moment, you saw a universe far beyond your misery and vowed to live.

Oh, the details may have been different. You would use other words. But you know the experience of divine intervention, when events in your life suddenly collided to put you on a new course. And you've been growing ever since, succeeding more and more, loving with more intensity than you ever could have imagined.

It's time now to repay the favor of God's love. Look around you. Who is in need of your touch, your special message? Whose life could be changed if only you would intervene with love? Look around . . . !

I joyously repay the favor love granted me.

Once, while filled with fear and misery,
love spoke to me and I was transformed.
My life is now about repaying the favor.

Denny LeClear

Altars are most often found in church. But, more and more, people are creating their own personal altars at home. It can be great fun and a form of practical spirituality. Honor the love you share and the goals for your future with a love altar.

Choose a private place, perhaps in your bedroom. It can be on the top of a low bookshelf, in a corner on the floor—wherever you have space to lay out a collection of meaningful and precious objects. Make sure they can't be disturbed by your kids or pets. Now incorporate photos of yourselves, love letters, heart-shaped objects. Maybe a picture of your future house, baby, car or puppy. Throw in some money and crystals or favorite stones for good luck. A few religious symbols. Change your altar as often as you please. Let your imagination soar.

Express your love. Create a sacred space dedicated to the two of you. Amen.

I will help us make an altar to honor love.

❧

Creating an altar in the home is saying
"This is what I value."

Ruth Barrett

Sometimes when you're out with friends, as a couple or alone, you may think it's very humorous to make fun of your husband, to take a sarcastic swipe at your wife. But it's not funny. It simply demonstrates that the two of you aren't taking care of your lovework in the privacy of your home. It makes you look juvenile. Your spouse feels hurt and embarrassed. And it adds more damage to whatever needs attention between the two of you.

If you agree to speak with friends about your marital difficulties, either do it together with another couple you both trust, or explain in advance that you will seek advice from a friend. Then bring back what you've learned so that both of you can benefit from it and your spouse doesn't feel left out.

Under no circumstances is it acceptable to put each other down in public. Respect yourself, your spouse and your friends enough to take care of your gripes in private.

I won't criticize my spouse in public.

⚜️

*My personal peeve is when spouses spout insults
about each other in front of their friends.*

Michael Webb

When you love someone you can easily develop your intuitive availability to one another. Your intuition is not just a spontaneous hunch, though that happens. More often it's your conscious ability to read your spouse's energy.

Right now notice the mood you're in. Sense the energy in your body. That's the energy that makes up your "energy body." Anyone who is tuned into you can sense what you're feeling. That's why your spouse may ask, "Are you alright?" and you've barely entered the room. Or they may sense your sexual interest before you're aware of your excitement.

Practice consciously tuning in to your spouse's energy. It can be very reassuring when your spouse is late and you scan for his energy out in the world, and you "know" all is well. Or she hasn't called yet, and you read her energy, and it's fine. Use your intuition to be even closer, intuitively closer to your love.

I trust my intuition as part of our relationship.

✕

Psychic empathy is the ability to sense the subtle energy around us. People are more than just their physical bodies. We all have energy fields that extend several feet beyond us and convey information.

Judith Orloff

Because we're so afraid that who we are isn't good enough, we often fail to show up and be present, particularly in our most intimate relationships. And sadly, it causes no end of trouble, pain and confusion.

You see, you are teachers and learners together in creating your marriage. And you can't do that very well unless the lesson plans are spelled out clearly. So, make this commitment to your partner and to yourself: I will straightforwardly tell you my needs and concerns at all times. No manipulating, no games, no techniques. Just put yourself out there so you and your spouse can deal with whatever's going on. Don't wheedle, don't cajole. Just say what the issue is.

Pretty strange, huh? Speaking up is the most important vow? Yes. Without your truth, without your full presence, you cannot create a loving relationship. With it, you have the freedom of deep trust and openness that will see you through any of life's challenges. Just show up!

I bless my love by showing up.

Eighty percent of success is just showing up.
Woody Allen

When you open yourself to the power of love, you begin to experience the Magic of the Universe. It becomes clear that loving energies, loving connections produce by-products and outcomes in your relationship and in your life that otherwise could not be expected.

As you give yourself over to love, you invite the Powers That Be to dance with you in ways that were never before permitted. As long as you thought you controlled everything, there was no room for magic. And so it could never appear. But openhearted love moves you beyond control, into the realms of spirit. Then, and only then, do you invite the presence of magic to play with you.

Open yourself to magic—the magic of the unexpected gift, the unsought raise, the unsuspected thrill of a new personal connection, even an unwanted move to a new town—almost anything can lead you into realms of love and success. Now, that's magic!

**I believe in the magic of forces
outside my own will.**

*Magic is the relationship
we have with divine energy.*

Phyllis Curott

We're never too old to enjoy a loving treat. Never. If you think you are, it's not your age. It's just toughness disguising your tender heart.

Make your love an everyday holiday! Open up your imagination. Tuck a stuffed bear into her luggage where she'll find it when she unpacks: "I'm thinking about snuggling with you." Deliver a plant to his office: "You're growing on me!" Buy special spices for the exotic food she loves. Check out his closet and buy his favorite kind of shirt. Put a heart sticker in his organizer to be found later.

Surprises break up the routine of your life. They say "I love you" when you can't be together. And they're great fun both to give and receive.

I love giving and receiving romantic surprises.

We surprise each other all the time in
both large and small ways.

Barbara Steffin and Nick Rath

How often do we try to shortchange love? We "make do" with bargains, we live together in a thrown-together home, refusing to stretch ourselves to provide the Godiva Chocolate version of love.

What are you waiting for when you serve up half-baked versions of love? Do you expect it will be Tom Cruise or Gloria Estefan that gets your best? Come on, face it: Julia Roberts and Will Smith aren't available—even if you'd get out the "good china" for them.

True love doesn't have a bargain rate. It loves with full value, and expects that you do the same—emotionally and even materially. Okay, you grew up learning to go without. Understandable. But don't keep doing it today. Especially not emotionally. Give and receive rich Rocky Road love every day. Once in awhile even go for the Hot Fudge Sundae version—or even the Three-Flavor-Banana-Split-with-a-Cherry-on-Top kind of love. Now you're talkin'.

I want value, not inferior bargains.

Buy the kind of ice cream that I like,
not the bad-taste, good-price kind.

Arthur, age eight

As humans we live with an ongoing need for growth and change. That urge is often stifled in childhood, when we're required to obey parents and teachers. So now, as adults, it can be a challenge to manifest what we want.

In order to manifest more love in your life, your focus needs to be creative, rather than acquisitive or grasping. This is a crucial distinction. In the creative realm, you enter into the spirit of what you want. When you're out to acquire or own something, you just go after it and get it. Love always wants to be attracted, not purchased, not grabbed on to.

Today, focus on living within the spirit of love, with no concern for the outcome. Notice how people treat you. Notice if your spouse seems more available when you allow the spirit of love to express through you more fully. Open yourself each day to living in the spirit of joyous love. You will become a magnet for what you want!

I manifest more and more love in my life.

When Spirit begins to rule in our lives,
we can literally manifest or attract to us everything
that we perceive to be missing.

Wayne Dyer

While you may not have time every morning, sharing your night's dreams can be a wonderfully intimate way to start your day. There's a magic to the journeys you take in your sleep that can help you with your daily living. When you discuss your dreams together, sharing them back and forth, you can get an even wider range of interpretations to help you understand their meaning. If you don't remember any dreams, share how you feel in your body and in your mood.

The goal is not to overanalyze your dreams, but to enjoy the romance of being so open and revealing, to trust each other with the inner language of your dreaming. Holding each other, looking at one another, feeling the deep bond of your sharing . . . what a wondrous way to start the day.

Even if you can only share your dreams on weekends, make the time to learn about one another this way. It adds a deeper dimension to your intimacy and to your dreaming.

**I enjoy getting to know my spouse
through our dreams.**

*It's so wonderful to cuddle, look into each other's eyes,
and share our night dreams with one another.*

Mark R. Harris

376

What did you learn growing up about how to think about and treat people who were different from you? Most people learned stuff like, "You can only trust your family," "Be polite, but don't marry one," "They're morons, stay away" and "Birds of a feather flock together." Stereotypes and prejudices served up in Dad's humor and snuck into Mom's apple pie.

Hatred and fear of differences are bred in the assumption that only our way counts, that we have "the right way." Every one of us is guilty. So each of us can help turn this around by opening up the way we look at differences.

When you see a woman with a "weird" hairdo, catch your judgment. Replace it with curiosity about what she sees in the mirror. The next time your spouse laughs "too loud," open your appreciation for her enthusiasm, his diverse humor. Teach your children that differences are part of the rich complexity of life. They'll love you for it.

I teach by loving the magic of differences.

*Parents need to learn how not to instill
snobby or holier-than-thou attitudes or preconceived
notions or stereotypes about other people. A child will
learn to internalize [the parents' attitudes].*

Sylvia Morelos

There comes a point in the journey of love when you are required to choose how you will love. Most people choose to commit themselves to the legal and spiritual requirements of marriage. Love is no longer just fun, passionate and delicious. It is now a profound choice.

In marriage, you won't always feel the warm bond, the hot passions of romantic love, but you can always choose love. You may feel tempted to dally with someone else, but you can choose to bring your commitment back home. You may feel like just giving in to your spouse to make some conflict go away, but you can choose to love yourself and your relationship enough to bring your needs and passions even more fully into the mix.

When love is your spiritual choice, there is no back door. There is no halfway commitment. You choose love, and only love. And it chooses you right back!

I embrace the morality of love.

❧

Love is a choice, but not always an easy choice.
Love is about choosing morals, ethics, passion and desire
without compromising your own character.

Laurie and Denny LeClear

You had lots of ideas about how married life was going to be, didn't you? And you've put lots of time and energy into trying to get it to match the picture, right? Well, what if you could have an even better marriage and feel even more loved if you gave up trying so hard? If you surrendered your attempts to control it all?

You've probably heard about "the zone," that state of mind where life just seems to flow—without effort. When athletes are "in the zone," they can do no wrong. Every pitch is a strikeout, every pass a touchdown. Well, love can be like that too.

To enter the zone, you have to have basic love skills—respect for differences, speaking up, listening, conflict resolution and receiving love. You have to be willing to have love change you. And you have to surrender to the flow of life. Let go!

I will give up trying to control love.

*When love takes you beyond
the need to control life,
you enter the zone and life begins to flow.*

Melody Starr

How many times have you watched an older couple out having breakfast? And you marvel as not a single word passes between them. They became stuck along the way, gave up and chose to spend their years together in frozen time.

But that's a choice. Born, perhaps, of ignorance, but a choice just the same. Make a different choice. Choose to get to know each other every day, in some new way.

When you stay open, the next phase of life will invite you to enter—together. You seek from each other support for greater courage and a wider spiritual stride, bolder creative edge. Together you ebb and flow as love moves you through serial monogamy with the dearly beloved person that you married all those precious years ago.

**I can have many different relationships
with my spouse.**

*Love is different things at different times
and in different circumstances.*

Paula Payne Hardin

Your marriage exists at a time when we are going through seismic shifts in consciousness—from "kill or get killed" to "my way or the highway" to "we can work it out"—and war is a primitive, obsolete stupidity.

How you conduct your marriage is not an isolated event. You will either contribute to human spiritual and intellectual progress or you'll add to the drag of the old ways. So, you don't want more pressure in your life, but you get the weight of the world dropped right on your shoulders. And it's true. Because we're all in this together. It's time we really get it. Each one of us is as important as any other and we need each other. The harmony of different notes is what makes the richest music, not one note repeated over and over.

It's time that we live as sisters and brothers in one family —the human race—and conduct our marriages as we want all people to treat one another. Peace!

I know it's time to release my fears and love fully.

It is time to end the division and to find harmony, whoever we are.

Ehud Barak

More and more, couples have different spiritual or religious beliefs. Some go to different churches or practice separate spiritual rituals. This can be quite wonderful, as long as both people openheartedly support one another's ways.

Before this century everyone pretty much stayed in their family community. Typically they married someone from the family church. But today we move around, meeting people with very different religious backgrounds. We're exposed to vastly different ideas about God and how to best live in spiritual harmony with God's teachings. The more we know, the more we see there are lots of different "teachings" that people adhere to.

Each of us must come to our own understanding of God, Yahweh, the Great Spirit or even atheism. If we are secure in our own faith, we are not threatened by someone else's beliefs. Keep your heart open to your lover's ways and rejoice in a God that is so large, so confident, that there's no one way to live in Grace.

I respect our differing spiritual needs and practices.

*We need our lover to understand our spiritual and religious
needs and to accept our way of manifesting them.*

Riki Robbins

A dmiring your spouse is quite different from liking him or enjoying her. When you admire the one you love, you sort of stand back and see the qualities you'd brag about if you were recommending her for a promotion, or pitching his story to a movie producer. It's all the stuff that garners your respect, makes you beam with pride!

How often do you tell your spouse how much you admire him? Why you admire her? If it's seldom, why are you being so stingy? And don't fall back on the quibble that no one's been bragging on you lately. That won't cut it.

Start noticing when you admire your spouse's integrity, honesty, ambition, great parenting, green thumb, intelligence, you name it. Whatever it is, take note inside your heart and then let your partner know how much you're filled with admiration and why. Make sure your spouse receives your gift of admiration!

Every day I find reason to openly admire my love.

The admiration between two people is the
most powerful support system a relationship can have,
the most powerful foundation.

Nathaniel Branden

L ove is just supposed to come along and fill you up, right? Well, it doesn't work that way. You see, love has to have someplace to welcome it. Someplace where it can feel at home.

If you routinely convince yourself of your worthlessness, then there's no room in your heart for love to reside. No matter how often or intensely your spouse gives you love, it can't get inside. It won't. Because you can't receive it. Now, that's no reason to feel hopeless or victimized. In fact, those are the feelings love wants you to give up.

In order to have space for love, you must develop your own self-worth. Begin by noticing the compliments people give to you. Don't push them away. Practice receiving them. Take them in and swallow them. Make them part of yourself. With practice, you'll be ready to receive the greater love of your spouse.

To receive love, I must value myself.

⁂

Only those who have, receive.

Joseph Roux

To experience the phenomenal experience of sacred sex, you both need to be emotionally available and have ample time to explore one another at leisure. Once you are comfortable, gradually bring into your sexuality the presence of the Divine—in yourself and in your partner.

Begin by looking into one another's eyes. Feel the deep love and intimacy you share. As you touch each other, keep in mind that you are an expression of God's love. Let sacred sex guide your physical connection. Through your touching you are offering a blessing, a sacrament expressed through the spirit and through the flesh. Know that your lover is an earthly expression of God's love as well. Your touch honors and celebrates the sacred beauty of your beloved's body, spirit and soul.

When you are being touched, receive the anointing as a sanctification of your personal love and of the Great Love that blesses all life on Earth. Now sex is a prayer of love.

To honor love I explore sacred sex.

Phenomenal sex means phenomenal love:
Love yourself, your partner, your world and Creator.
Be sexy from the deep inside out!

Marcia Singer

Have you noticed that when you're inspired by love, you shine at your very brightest? Your imagination is set on fire. Your generosity opens to new limits. You're effortlessly swept into the effort it will take to produce what you want. It doesn't matter if love moves you to help your favorite charity, write your first novel, plant a spring garden, or raise your child with tenderness and grace. Love moves you to do your very best, to give without thought to self-centered needs. That is your genius!

In your romantic relationship, follow your love genius. Let it move your actions, your creativity, your willingness to receive. So many people block their genius, fearful that if they give too much they will be taken advantage of, they'll get used. But love is not stupid. Your genius will not let you be mistreated. Only neurotic impulses do that.

Be your genius today. Let love guide your actions. Even at work, be a brilliant, shining star.

When I love, I tap into my genius.

❧

Love, love, love,
that is the soul of genius.

Wolfgang Amadeus Mozart

How much love and affection do you want? Or does that sound like a silly question? You want as much as you can get, right? Yet, if that's true for everyone, why is the divorce rate so high? Why are so many people discouraged about love?

Deeply intimate love takes lovework and time to develop. But many people give up long before love has an opportunity to ripen. They don't believe they deserve love. Or it's meant for others, or maybe it's not even real. So they settle for a pale companionship in the name of marriage, believing that's all there is.

You can only have the kind of love you believe in and work for. Don't shortchange your marriage by giving up as soon as you make an effort and change doesn't happen immediately. Hold the vision of what you want. Every day, move in that direction. Celebrate the new pleasures, the new intimacies. Trust that, in time and with effort, you'll grow into what you imagine. Enjoy the journey!

I can have a life of loving abundance.

All prosperity begins in the mind and is dependent only
upon the full use of our creative imagination.

Ruth Ross

How do you treat your best friend? Do you hold back information about yourself, what you like/what you don't? Do you decide alone what the two of you will do? Do you talk about her behind her back? Do you blow up at him over every disappointment? Probably not.

Yet, many people treat their spouse in ways that prohibit the foundation of deep friendship. Why? Because the dream of effortless, ecstatic romance has destroyed the possibility of liking each other, of wanting to be best friends. For a marriage to last over a lifetime, deep friendship must be the basis for love. You can have all the fairy-tale romance in the world, but without friendship, your love will die from neglect and exhaustion.

Today, treat your spouse as you would your best friend. Don't worry about sex or romance. Just focus on being the very best friend you know how to be. As the friendship deepens, your sexuality and romance will blossom!

Every day I become a better friend to my spouse.

Now I know that love is all about time, understanding, being best friends with each other.

Niki Taylor

Whatever you understand God to be, or however you comprehend your existence, the fact is that your presence here is a miracle. Just for starters, there has never, ever been another you and there never will. You are distinctly unique—different from all other humans—for all time.

Therefore, your primary spiritual challenge is to accept yourself as you are. Not what you've been told about who you are by parents, teachers, religious authorities or others, but to accept who you are underneath all the idealization or negativity. That means you get to liberate yourself from "original sin." Of course, if you choose original sin, go ahead. But why would your God want to have you express his/her creation by starting out as a sinner?

You were created to express some portion of the vastness of God's reality. Do it fully, do it well. Stop comparing yourself to others. Theirs is not your path. Step into your path fully and discover the miracle that is you.

**Accepting myself is the greatest gift
I can give to God.**

*I realized that when I embraced who I really was,
I became the best version of myself.*

Gwyneth Paltrow

Gifts and parties, and more gifts. But what gift survives the season? The gift of love. The gift of your blessing penetrates deep into the soul, lifting up all who receive it. It is not a foil-wrapped present, but rather the fullness of your loving presence. That is your true and timeless gift.

Any time you bestow a wish for goodness onto anyone or anything, you use the power of the sacred to benefit all of life. You claim your rightful place as a creator, as a maker of light and beauty. It is not for you to judge how others live, only to send them your openhearted wish for their well-being, success and happiness.

You may wish to speak your desire for someone's health, abundance, successful marriage or whatever, or you may just extend your blessing as a thought-form that will encircle them with a magic moment of grace. Your blessing is a gift of God. Give it with the fullness of your heart.

I bless all of life every day.

❧

To bless means to wish, unconditionally, total,
unrestricted good for others and events from the deepest
wellspring in your heart. . . . To bless all without discrimination
of any sort is the ultimate form of giving.

Pierre Pradervand

D o you relate to marriage in the same way you bake a cake or change the oil in your car: go through the process, then it's "Been there, done that, what next"? Well, that's fine for a cake or your car, but not for affairs of the heart. Love needs your attention and care for always. Once you've found it, never let it go to waste by taking it for granted.

When couples do this, they complain they're bored or have gone their different ways—allowing their love to wither and die from neglect. They've failed to be alert, on a daily basis, to the enchantment and cherishment love yields.

When you love for always, there is no end to rejoicing, no end to increasing your capacity to feel blessed by one another's sheer presence. Whenever you catch yourself in the doldrums, wake up: You've abandoned "alert" in favor of "numb." Today, open yourself to be constantly alert to the lifelong, continually unfolding fortune of love.

I commit to love for always.

❧

Love is that vital essence that pervades
and permeates from the center to the circumference,
the graduating circles of all thought and action.
Love is the talisman of human weal and woe—
the open sesame to every soul.

Elizabeth Cady Stanton

A s you love, so shall you grace us all. Give yourself to the fullness of life and you bless the entire world. Your generosity moves outward into an arc of goodwill upon all that you encounter. Yours is the power to bring love, light and hope where there is none—if only for a moment.

The light you are willing to shine may touch someone who wants to shine but would not do so until you did. And now there is another who touches another and then another—none of which may have happened but for you.

Light is like that. It passes through resistances and softens boundaries, ingesting the darkness until, finally, there is a new dawn. Shine, radiance, shine. That is your power and your virtue. That is your essence. So, shine! Shine!

I am a radiant being.

As Sunlight must be reflected upon an Object to be seen ...
Life is the Object that reflects the Light of Your Being....
May Your Light Know No Boundary.

Brian Cochrane

You may not know it, but you are a leader. To whatever degree you refuse to follow others, to follow old prescribed ways, to live without deciding on your own path, you are a leader. In the realm of love, there is still much to be learned. It is your search to know more of love that leads others.

Do not take your leadership lightly. What may seem like a small thing to you may be revolutionary to someone else. Refusing to backstab at work, never putting your spouse down in public—these are models for respectful living. But go further. When you make a point of smiling, praising good work and congratulating promotions, you advance the voice of love. When you and your spouse hold hands and dance lovingly with each other at a party, you show the way to more romance and better marriage.

Open your imagination to see how you can lead. Where can you open your heart in public and show the way?

I show the way to new regions of loving.

Do not follow where the path may lead.
Go instead where there is no path,
and leave a trail.

Anonymous

L ove, real love, brings out the best in us. When we are available to love and be loved, there is a fullness of being that leads us out beyond our self-centered concerns as we extend to embrace a wider and wider world.

What could be a better arena for this kind of soul work than marriage? The differences between two people, and the challenges they provide, compel us to consider the otherness of our spouse. They also offer an ongoing variety of experiences that lead us beyond what we could have ever imagined. When we take up our lovework, we give a gift of will and commitment to the soul that returns to us a connection to the infinite.

So, that is what your relationship offers: nothing less than a bridge from the infinite below to the infinite above, from what is within you to that which is around you, from the mundane to the sacred—from life to love to God.

I dedicate myself to the lovework of the soul.

※

Relationship . . . was created as your perfect
tool in the work of the soul.

Neale Donald Walsch

L ife can be very hard. Very unfair. It's easy to get lost in bitter insistence that it shouldn't be that way. When you reject what is, all that love has to offer is out of reach, beyond your imagination.

Fortunately we are blessed with the opportunity to exceed the trials of a seemingly harsh reality and open to the transcendent forces of love. We can feel the pain of loss, disappointment, even tragedy, and at the same time experience the larger reality of love in our lives. We can remember that each of us is part of the Whole of Life, that none of us is actually separated from one another on the spiritual plane of existence.

For today, concentrate on love. No matter what issues may arise, remember to view the situation through the eyes of love. Keeping your heart open, notice how you can transcend the vagaries of everyday life and turn your participation into a prayer of love.

I can see love in everything.

One word
Frees us of all the weight and pain of life:
LOVE.

Sophocles

Is it clear to you that your relationship will take you into your final years? Oh, yes, of course, no one has any guarantee of what the future will hold. But, assuming you're both alive in your nineties or even beyond, can you look forward to still holding hands?

Or does the thought of aging together frighten you? You'd rather not think about it? That's a choice, but it's part of the love life you can share now.

Consider how much richer your commitment might be today if you included in your awareness the certainty that you will still be sweethearts in your last years—that you will embrace the end as much as the beginning of your love. That you will still be growing and learning about love, even as the time will come to say, "Good-bye, my most precious blessing. I've loved living my life with you. May we meet on the other side."

I look forward to our last years together.

❧

Both Garry [Trudeau] and I totally take for granted
that we're going to be old people together.

Jane Pauley

The end of a year. A good year. A year of spiritual adventure and lessons of love. A year of challenges and great delights. You're not the same as you were one year go. Yes, it was a very good year.

And now a new year is soon to begin. As you cast your shadow on the departing twelve months, what future awaits? It is yours for the making; don't make it in haste.

Spend this, the final day of this good year, in private prayer for the next year. Open up wide to the possibilities. For God needs clear room to dance and play in your dreams.

I make this day a prayer for the New Year.

For yesterday is but a dream,
And tomorrow is only a vision:
But today well-lived makes
Every yesterday a dream of happiness,
And every tomorrow a vision of hope.
Look well therefore to this day!
Such is the salutation of the dawn!

Sanskrit poem

Happy New Year to you
With our love, Judith & Jim

The basic discovery about any people is the discovery of the relationship between its men and women.

Pearl S. Buck

The Magic of Differences

Creating a New Understanding Between Men and Women

Judith and Jim founded their company, The Magic of Differences, in 1988. They have helped thousands of people realize that it's the differences between two people in relationship that offer the deepest intimacy, the richest passion and the most powerful opportunities for emotional and spiritual growth. Judith and Jim provide lectures, workshops and audiotapes for singles and couples to help them open to the richness of real love.

They provide weekend relationship trainings called "The New Intimacy: How to Create Real Romance in Your Everyday Life" for couples and singles. Judith and Jim are approved to offer a range of CEU classes, among them The New Intimacy, which is approved for fifteen hours of MCEP credit by the CPA Accrediting Agency, provider #SHE013.

As consultants and trainers they address the changing

gender culture in public and private life, working with professional associations, nonprofit organizations, churches and corporations. Their corporate clients have included Unocal, The Walt Disney Company, The W. K. Kellogg Foundation, Pepperdine University, St. John's Hospital, National Academy of Songwriters and Catholic Charities.

They produce, market and distribute their own lecture and guided-meditation audiotape series entitled "Reclaiming the Self" and a personal workshop audiotape series titled "The Love Made Simple Program."

Please contact Judith and Jim for information about speaking engagements, workshops, training programs, newsletter and audiotapes or to schedule them for a presentation.

Judith & Jim
The Magic of Differences
12021 Wilshire Blvd. PMB 692
Los Angeles, CA 90025
(310) 829-3353; Fax (310) 829-4927
jimjude@ix.netcom.com

You can also learn more about Judith and Jim's work or order their books and tapes from their World Wide Web page at:

http://*www.thenewintimacy.com*

Excite@Home

All brand. All device. All the time.

Wisdom Radio . . . Programming that can change your life.

You can listen to their talk-radio show daily from 3–5 P.M. (ET) and noon–2 P.M. (PT) *www.wisdomradio.com*

We wish you the magic of love and intimacy in your real, everyday life.

About the Authors

Husband and wife psychology team, Judith Sherven, Ph.D., and James Sniechowski, Ph.D., are two of the country's pioneering most respected, and sought-after authorities on relationship dynamics. Their bestselling first book, *The New Intimacy: Discovering the Magic at the Heart of Your Differences* (Health Communications, Inc., 1997), and their lectures, workshops and trainings continue to change the lives of couples and singles, awakening them to a new vision of intimate relationship, and helping them discover the rich spiritual purpose for the challenges of real-life love.

They are acclaimed for their groundbreaking work in the study and understanding of differences in relationships and how to turn those differences into exciting catalysts for heightened intimacy in marriage, better communication in dating and greater respect and understanding in any relationship.

Judith is a clinical psychologist and was the founding director of the Institute for Advanced Training in Experiential

Psychotherapy, and has been a psychotherapist in private practice since 1978. Jim holds a doctorate in Human Behavior and is the founder and director of the Menswork Center in Santa Monica, California, and a cofounder of the Men's Health Network in Washington, D.C. As an international leader and speaker on men's issues, he provides workshops, men's groups and individual consultation.

Judith and Jim are frequently called upon by the media as experts in their field. They have appeared on over 500 television and radio talk shows, including *The Oprah Winfrey Show, The View, This Evening with Judith Regan, The O'Reilly Factor, New Attitudes, 48 Hours, Entertainment Tonight* and *Leeza,* and on the Fox News Channel, CNN and MSNBC News with Brian Williams.

They can be heard Monday through Friday, noon–2 P.M. (PT) on their talk-radio show, syndicated nationally by Wisdom Radio. They invite their audience to look at issues that bear directly on the lives they live with those they love. Judith and Jim look for the heart and soul behind the headlines, bringing to talk radio a new approach— one that cares instead of swears. You can log on to *www.wisdomradio.com.*

They have written for or been interviewed by *The Los Angeles Times, USA Today, Chicago Tribune, San Francisco Chronicle, London Sunday Times, The Wall Street Journal, Redbook, Essence, First for Women, Black Elegance, Playboy, Today's Black Woman, Black Men* and *Family Circle.*

More than their extensive professional background, Judith and Jim bring a personal, down-to-earth approach to their work. They live in Santa Monica and have been married for twelve years. It's Judith's first and Jim's third marriage. They bring hope for almost everybody!

THE NEW INTIMACY
Exploring the space between us!

THE LATEST CHICKEN SOUP FOR THE SOUL

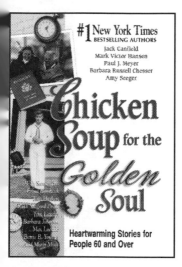

Chicken Soup for the Golden Soul

Celebrating the myriad joys of living and the wisdom that comes from having lived, this collection offers loving insights and wisdom—all centering on the prime of life. You will be sure to cherish these invaluable stories as a reminder that the soul of those young at heart is truly "golden." Code # 7257 Quality Paperback - $12.95

Chicken Soup for the Christian Family Soul

This inspiring volume celebrates wholesome, traditional values and principles. Themes of forgiveness, faith, hope, charity and love will lift your spirits, deepen your faith and expand your awareness of how to practice Christian values in your daily life—at home, at work and in the community.

Code #7141 Quality Paperback - $12.95

Selected titles also available in hardcover, large print, audiocassette and CD. Prices do not include shipping and handling. Available in bookstores everywhere or call **1.800.441.5569** for Visa or MasterCard orders. Your response code is **BKS**. Order online at *www.bci-online.com*